DESIGNING PERFORMANCE APPRAISALS

ASSESSING NEEDS AND DESIGNING PERFORMANCE
MANAGEMENT SYSTEMS IN THE PUBLIC SECTOR

Published by: Commonwealth Secretariat
                 Marlborough House
                 Pall Mall
                 London SW1Y 5HX
                 UNITED KINGDOM

May be purchased from:

Publications Unit
Commonwealth Secretariat

Telephone: +44 (0) 20 7747 6342
Facsimile: +44 (0) 20 7839 9081

ISBN: 0 85092 630 0

Price: £9.00/$14.00

Printed by Dudley Print

DESIGNING PERFORMANCE APPRAISALS

ASSESSING NEEDS AND DESIGNING PERFORMANCE MANAGEMENT SYSTEMS IN THE PUBLIC SECTOR

Edited by

Sam Agere

Noella Jorm

Management and Training Services Division

Commonwealth Secretariat

FOREWORD

A strong and achieving public service is a necessary condition for a competitively successful nation. The Management and Training Services Division (MTSD) of the Commonwealth Secretariat assists member governments to improve the performance of the public service through action-oriented advisory services, policy analysis and training. This assistance is supported by funds from the Commonwealth Fund for Technical Co-operation (CFTC).

Commonwealth co-operation in public administration is facilitated immeasurably by the strong similarities that exist between all Commonwealth countries in relation to the institutional landscape and the underlying principles and values of a neutral public service. In mapping current and emerging best practices in public service management, MTSD has been able to draw on the most determined, experienced and successful practitioners, managers, and policy-makers across the Commonwealth. Their experiences point the way to practical strategies for improvement.

The publication series, Managing the Public Service: Strategies for Improvement, provides the reader with access to the experiences and successes of newly designed or reformed performance management systems across the Commonwealth.

Many organisations are under pressure both from internal and external sources to improve their performance and achieve the set goals and objectives. Performance management has consequently become a popular concept in the meaningful and effective utilisation of human, financial, material and organisational resources for the benefit of the public, customers and users of the service. In order to implement performance management systems, goals and objectives must be clearly defined, performance measures identified and accountability for meeting performance expectations ensured. In developing performance management systems, the critical questions that have often been raised are: How do you measure performance? How do you identify performance indicators and, above all, How do you design performance appraisal systems?

This publication is a major contribution to the ways and means of designing performance appraisal systems as a result of the public sector reforms taking place in almost all Commonwealth countries. This publication also raises serious questions for debate, issues to be further addressed and suggestions on how to design and institutionalise performance management measures into the organisational culture, systems, structures, processes and procedures.

Michael Gillibrand
Acting Director and Special Adviser
Management and Training Services Division

ACKNOWLEDGEMENTS

The Commonwealth Secretariat is grateful to Sam Agere, the Special Adviser on Management Development in the Commonwealth Fund for Technical Co-operation, and to Noella Jorm, an independent performance management consultant based in Sydney, Australia, the co-authors of this publication. Special thanks are due to the following contributors: Mr Selwyn Smith, a former Permanent Secretary for the Ministry of the Public Sector Reform in the Government of Barbados, who prepared the Barbados Experience; Dr Matagialofi Luaiufi-Moli, the Secretary of the Public Service Commission in the Government of Samoa (South Pacific), who contributed the Samoa Experience; and the Chief Establishment Officer in the Government of Tonga, who provided the material from which it was possible to compile the performance management system in that country.

Thanks are also due to Roy Chalmers, Greg Covington and Ivy Chikoti for their assistance in the production of this publication.

Although in editing, every attempt has been made to retain the accuracy of the contributions, the final responsibility for any errors or inaccuracies rests with the Commonwealth Secretariat.

ACKNOWLEDGEMENTS

CONTENTS

INTRODUCTION

Performance management is a concept that has come into popular use in the management of an organisation's human, material and financial resources for the benefit of the public or consumers. Globally defined performance management is the use of performance measurement in shaping the performance of organisations and people. Many leading organisations use performance measurement – the process of assessing progress towards achieving predetermined goals – to gain insight into, and make judgements about, the effectiveness and efficiency of their programmes, processes and people.

Performance management can perhaps be described as the use of performance measurement information to:

- evaluate performance in achieving performance goals;
- allocate and prioritise resources;
- provide managers with information to confirm or alter the measured performance.

Operating within the framework of a clear and consistent management system, high-performing organisations seeking to implement performance management systems must first establish:

- clear performance measures;
- define performance goals and communicate expectations; and
- ensure accountability for meeting performance expectations.

Implementing successful performance management systems requires not only gathering and analysing data according to predetermined processes, but also utilising that information to affect performance. The development and implementation of a successful performance management system implies that organisations use performance Information in a systematic manner to impact decisions throughout an organisation. (International Symposium on Public Personnel Management, 1998).

Clearly, it is important to understand what has to be measured and to determine the performance factors such as financial considerations, internal business operations, customer satisfaction, employee satisfaction and community/ stakeholder satisfaction. The next step is to identify a baseline and determine a goal for each of the measures selected. When performance measures have been developed and the performance goals set, a method of regular review of the established performance measures must be determined. However, continuous and regular review measures, as they relate to the corresponding goals and the organisation's strategic plan are key to the success of any performance management system. In all these stages, the leadership, management and employees must understand the processes, procedures and practices that have been agreed upon. The involvement of all managers and employees in determining the type of measurement required, is necessary in order to make them committed to its success and for them to own the process as this is linked to the rewards or pay to the performance measurement system.

SOCIO-ECONOMIC AND ORGANISATIONAL ENVIRONMENT

BACKGROUND

Increasingly, many Commonwealth countries face a continued need to improve the ways in which public administration operates. The most immediate challenge for improvement comes from the demands that are created by attempts to respond and adjust to the new economic policies, social development strategies and managerial systems. The transformation for example, from planned economies and rigid bureaucratic structures to flexible, needs-driven management also creates further demands.

Faced by the demands and challenges of responding to national and international issues, policy-makers and managers have recognised the need to progress towards sustainable development. The process of making and implementing policy, however, requires skills and techniques to review and evaluate existing policy as well as to design and develop organisational systems and structures. The increase in public demand for better services and improved delivery systems has made it imperative that ways and means of working differently and producing the desired results are found. The continued dwindling of resources and the corresponding increase in the demand for better quality services have placed enormous pressure on management to identify appropriate approaches, methods and practices to effective and efficient ways of utilising available resources.

These pressures have led managers to focus on increasing productivity and improving the performance of public service delivery systems. Consequently, a performance management system has been identified as one of the ways of improving the provision of services and increasing productivity. It is therefore conceptualised in a socio-economic and organisational environment within which it functions.

The aim of this public action is first of all an attempt to respond to these pressures for improvement in the provision of services at three levels namely, national, organisation and individual. As a concept, a performance management system constitutes:

1. ***Performance Agreement:*** the need to identify and agree on the role, stating what is to be achieved and how success will be measured, identifying key relationships and suggesting improvement plans.

2. ***Performance Appraisal:*** jointly assessing performance, agreeing any development needs, and agreeing goals for next appraisal period.

3. ***Performance Coaching***: on-going coaching by managers throughout the year. This includes monitoring counselling and discipline process.

4. ***Performance Rewards***: whether pay and promotion are tied to the performance appraisal or not, employees who perform well expect to be rewarded. Rewards can take the form of material awards like pay increases, promotion or bonuses and can also be in the form of recognition.[1]

The second aim of this publication is to contribute to the on-going attempts being made to design performance appraisal instruments to suit particular countries, states, organisations and employers and employees.

The third aim is to demonstrate how to measure performance in the delivery of public service to the people. It may sound simple to talk about measuring tangible products but it is not easy to measure results which are abstract, which cannot be quantified and which are a part of a process of delivery. In order to measure the abstract, there must always be an agreement on what, how and when to measure. Such an agreement can become complicated in situations where objectivity is difficult to realise.

The fourth aim is to discuss how performance management systems can be institutionalised and be made part of an organisation's culture. Training, transfer of skills and the involvement of employees in the formulation as well as in the implementation of management systems constitute part of a global approach to the inculcation of management values and ethics.

The discussion on the performance appraisal instrument is exemplified by the three case studies from Barbados (Caribbean), Samoa and Tonga (South Pacific), all of which represent the small island states within the Commonwealth of nations.

The overall approach to the subject of performance appraisal is first to conduct a needs assessment, secondly to design an appropriate instrument, thirdly to train the users of the instrument and lastly to install the instrument in the public service machinery. All these approaches and techniques are considered in the context of the global economic political and social circumstances. The pressures for change will be identified and the current practices and procedures will be analysed.

The essential lessons to be drawn from designing and installing the appraisal instrument, through the direct involvement of the employees and managers alike are:

1. ***Promoting individual learning through doing things for themselves***
    Individual learning takes place on the job and in the work place – the lessons of experience that result from key work assignments, dealings with colleagues and superiors, organisational successes and mistakes. Individuals are ultimately responsible for their own learning because only the learner can learn, no matter how much others support or help the process.

2. ***Organisational learning*** The goal is to enhance the performance of the organisation and the quality of life within it. The benefits of individual learning will never become organisational benefits unless the organisation itself can provide the culture and circumstances to translate individual learning into organisational thought and practice. Organisations are therefore responsible for creating the conditions under which individual insights and understandings can be absorbed by the organisation itself and can begin to shape its course.

3. ***Instilling the culture of continuous learning*** in order to improve operational performance at a practical level. This can be achieved through:

    ▪ Benchmarking – comparing the organisation with other organisations known for their efficiency or effectiveness, identifying and adapting their best practices to improve one's performance.

    ▪ Identifying ways to work faster and more simply by eliminating unnecessary steps and redundant work that adds no value.[2]

4.   *Inculcating appropriate values to employees*

- The values driving work practices relate to those behaviours and orientations which are identified as supportive of high levels of individual contribution and performance.

- Service-oriented values which highlight the need for respect of others, for supportive leadership and efficiency and effectiveness in the organisation in order to provide for innovative and quality services to clients and value to the community.

- Professionalism and conduct values which relate to factors that promote a high standard of personal conduct from individuals in the work place. Being effective in one's job by providing quality results is related to holding a strong sense of loyalty and commitment to one's colleagues and the organisation.

- Rights and duties values highlight the importance of being held accountable for the discharge of responsibilities in public office.

- Work-place democracy values – this set of values emphasises respect and caring for people as well as the involvement of others in the dialogue and decision-making process concerning work-related issues.[3]

The process of involving employees and their managers in designing the performance appraisal instrument inculcates a sense of ownership and assures a high degree of sustainability. It further simplifies the installation of the instrument and makes training and implementation more relevant to the peculiar needs and problems of the public service. Through working together, a culture of belonging to the public service emerges which in turn consolidates the commitment to the organisation.

Properly used, performance management is a strategic, integrating factor in reward and human resources development. It provides the sand and cement that binds the organisation together so that it can deliver its core purpose. It should be a seamless process that achieves greater overall value than the sum of its individual elements of objective setting, monitoring and appraising.

A variety of performance management approaches will often need to be accommodated, communicated and rewarded within the same organisation, depending on the tasks, stage of development and potential impact of its strategic business units.

To transform business goals into results, taking organisational reality into account, management should develop a performance management strategy. They should look at three aspects:

- Who is involved, the leaders or the led? In what ways do their interests coincide or conflict and where is the source of power?

- What do they want to achieve? Is it a short-term aim, does it have tangible or intangible parameters, and what are the key resources?

- Where are they situated in time and space? Does the organisationally or geographically determined culture have a positive or negative effect?

This perspective can help to establish whether particular approaches will fit an organisation's circumstances.

The performance management model for the post-industrial era emphasises cross-functional, self-directed teamwork in a flat structure. Its practitioners communicate using complex interpersonal relationships rather than rigid terminology. People demand leadership and coaching rather than management and supervision. Knowledge professionals are recognised and rewarded for contributing diverse creature and intellectual potential to help their organisations succeed in the search for investment and customers.

Many countries are already implementing various approaches to improved performance management as part of the overall economic and administrative reform. The advantages of the reform are being shared internationally through improved technology, knowledge, and skills. To this extent performance management has become part of the global village and hence is an effect of the globalisation process.

THE EFFECTS OF GLOBALISATION

Globalisation represents growing integration of the economic, financial, political, social and cultural lives of countries. Rapid globalisation has been induced by a scientific-technological revolution, by the need to reap the economies of scale of international markets and the unprecedented openness of states. It has simultaneously opened up a world of immense opportunities, challenges and risks for developing countries. As global needs for knowledge increase, the challenge for development learning institutions is to understand the dynamics of the learning process and to disseminate knowledge and information that embody some of the best practices and technology from around the world. At the same time, it is important that they remain closely attuned to the client so that services reflect needs, that programmes make the most of the available resources and help clients to address poverty and sustainable development.[4]

The challenge to developing countries in public sector reform, which has become one of the effects of globalisation, is not only to create more knowledge on performance management systems, but also to reinforce the capabilities – both human and institutional – to use the available knowledge effectively. The sharing and diffusion of ideas by Commonwealth countries is one of the ways to improve productivity at a national and organisational level. What is important with respect to performance management is that the international flow of ideas and techniques must relate to local needs, culture and level of development. Collaborative working partnerships among Commonwealth countries, which pool resources together to generate, share and disseminate knowledge are another important product. External knowledge networks are developed in co-operation with partner institutions that both contribute to and benefit from this type of association of Commonwealth members.

The rapid and inevitable diffusion of knowledge and information on performance management has been accompanied by evidence and benefits of utilising the instrument in expenditure reduction, prevention of corruption and attraction to investments. Hence, as a result of this diffusion of technology, many developing countries:

- elect to use the technology where appropriate;

- become proactive in designing such instruments in collaboration with donors and international organisations;

- have put in place as a matter of policy, performance management mechanisms;

- have focused on the needs of people rather than the global market only.

Performance management policies in many of the developing Commonwealth countries can be characterised by varying institutional intervention mechanisms.

There are about three ways in which performance management is being conceptualised and institutionalised:

1. *Strategic planning* This is the level of goal-setting and review of functions of ministries as part of the public sector reform programme. Strategic planning can be said to provide the level for top influence and is manifest in at least three forms:

    (a) A proactive intervention, where a government has an explicit policy on performance management and has set up an inter-ministerial committee on public sector reform. Top-down mobilisation represents a significant institutional intervention in promoting the reform programme downstream.

    (b) Reactive intervention, where a government has an implicit performance management policy and opts to be responsive, in the informal sense, to the recommendations of an *ad hoc* committee or professional body. Such intervention is prevalent in many developing Commonwealth countries.

    (c) A passive intervention, where government has no performance management policy, implicit or otherwise, but opts to let policy follow market forces, either by deliberate intention or by way of being at an initial stage of the reform programme.

2. *Co-ordination, promotion and control* This is the level of resource allocation, control and monitoring. The degree of effectiveness in the

implementation of the performance management policies and strategies depends very much on whether the leadership (political and administrative) is committed.

3.   ***Operational implementation level*** This is the level of execution of specific tasks and activities and compromise interventions by training institutions, regional and international organisations with special interest in user ministries and departments.[5]

The socio-political and economic changes taking place all over the world have a direct impact on the development agenda of each country. There is no country that is metaphorically an island of its own. Most countries belong to regional and international organisations. Consequently, each country is bound to be influenced by some of the change processes taking place in countries where it has common interests. However, the influence, good or bad, occurs despite the sovereign nature of the state.

These change processes are part of globalisation. While globalisation is not a new concept, it has, over the last decade, been considered a phenomenon taking place in world economic, political, social environmental systems. The wave of globalisation in the Eighties and Nineties has been driven by a set of factors such as deregulation, in particular, of the financial services, the emergence of new transportation and communication technologies, the collapse of the Eastern bloc and the demonstration effect of the success stories of the East Asian countries.

The globalisation process has different dimensions whose principal characteristics consist of the following:

- globalisation of the markets;

- the internationalisation of corporate strategies, in particular their commitment to competition as a source of wealth creation;

- the diffusion of technology and related research and development and knowledge world-wide;

- the transformation of consumption patterns into cultural products with world-wide consumer markets;

- the internationalisation of the regulatory capabilities of national societies into a global political economic system;

- the diminished role of national governments in designing the rules for global governance.[6]

It should be mentioned that not all the characteristics may occur at any one point in time. However, this book focuses on the changing role of the state in the management of human, financial and material resources of a country. The changing role is also heavily influenced by the diffusion in technology, transformation of consumption patterns into cultural products and the promotion of international standards. The liberalisation policies, the restructuring of organisations that deliver the services and the pressure for increased productivity amid reduced resources have, for example, had an impact in many countries. The pace for change differs from one country to another.

Although globalisation is a process of change, it is more often than not, driven by special problems, challenges and interests that surface from time to time in the economic and political space. Within globalisation there are therefore rules which guide behaviour and standards, which in turn institutionalise linkage aimed at strengthening the integration process of members.

Within the economic field, globalisation has resulted in the development of new markets; new tools, e.g. internet links; cellular phones; media networks; and new actors such as the World Trade Organisation (WTO) with authority over national governments; multinational corporations with more economic power than many states; global networks for non-governmental organisations (NGOs) and other groups that transcend national boundaries. In order to strengthen this process, new rules have been established, for example, multilateral agreements on trade, services and intellectual property, backed by strong enforcement mechanisms and more binding for national governments, reducing the scope for national policy.[7]

In addition to global markets and global technology are also global ideas and global solidarity, which can enrich the lives of people everywhere and consequently improve the management processes of development and productivity. The growing interdependence of peoples' lives calls for shared values, standards and shared commitment to the human development of all people.

The challenge of globalisation in the next century is to improve the power relationship, sharing equitably the proceeds from global markets, demonstrate social justice and improve human development. It should be guided by ethics, equity, inclusion, human security, sustainability, development and management. In order, for example, to improve efficiency and effectiveness in the delivery of service to the public, performance management principles and practices should be equally guided by such ethics and standards. These standards contribute to good governance at local, national, regional and international levels.

In instituting standards, there is an assumption that they must be objectively measured to ensure social justice and improve productivity. Performance management practices must therefore have procedures, rules, behaviour patterns and agreements on what objectives to achieve and within what time-frame and resources. Performance of the markets, technology, capital flow and development now requires that there be some measurements. More progress can be measured through norms, standards policies and institutions. Both organisations and individuals have an interest in developing objectives measurement of success, productivity, achievement of efficiency and effectiveness. Better performance practices can therefore be instrumental in improving the delivery of service to the public. If these performance practices are not in place, the effects of the global markets, technology and ideas will not be realised successfully at local levels.

The globalisation process is translated or transferred through some international organisations, multilateral agencies, bilateral and individual non-government organisations. However, international organisations have played a significant role in imparting global ideas to many countries. Although some of them have been subjected to intense scrutiny and criticism over the past decade, they have nevertheless a number of critical and catalytic roles in management of resources and public administration. International organisations enjoy a comparative advantage over national entities in that they:

- set global norms and standards governing information, regulation, legislation, best practices and ideas. Multilateral agencies are well placed to build knowledge networks with their links to member governments and academic institutions but, more importantly, can provide a comparatively neutral forum for debate;

- can provide global action and suggestions for ways of improving performance, fighting corruption and sharing technology which some countries may not be able to afford to buy. Examples include seminars in which experiences are shared and best practices formulated;

- facilitate financial and technical resource transfer. Multilateral agencies contribute substantially to development assistance, particularly to research into management studies, capacity building and improving the human resource base of an administration;[8]

- provide leadership training and support, particularly in managing public service reform process. Some ideas, for example, on privatisation, commercialisation and restructuring the economy, have been shared through international and regional conferences. Professional organisations such as the Commonwealth Association of Public Administration and Management (CAPAM), Commonwealth Local Government Forum (CLGF), Commonwealth Network of Information and Technology (COMNET-IT), Commonwealth Parliamentary Association (CPA) etc., are instrumental to the sharing of ideas, practices and latest developments in personnel management. They are, therefore, vehicles for globalisation through benchmarking, study tours, conferences exchange programmes and technical assistance.

International organisations that have been involved in public management include UNDP, Commonwealth Secretariat, African and Asian Development Banks and other organisations that support specific sectors such as health (WHO), education (UNESCO), labour (ILO), etc. In some countries there has been a proliferation of development with the result that there has been duplication of services and sometimes competition among donors.

Development assistance has also been provided through bilateral arrangements and co-operation between two countries. In other cases, some developed countries have been assisting small and poor countries in improving their human resource capacity and skills in financial management. Non-governmental organisations also contribute to individual countries in like manner. Whatever the form of assistance, the principal factor in the process of globalisation is the sharing of ideas and the transfer of knowledge and technology in order to improve the management of development resources. The ultimate beneficiaries of the transfer or sharing of resources are the people. Such transfer can only succeed if there are effective and proper procedures and processes of delivering the service. Furthermore, the measurement of performance on the delivery of service is important to both the donors and the recipients of service and assistance. In this regard, performance management and appraisal are instruments which must be regularly reviewed in order to ensure that they respond to the changing needs of society. While performance management in the present context is conceptualised as part of or an effect of globalisation process, it is also part of the reform of the public administrative system which, in turn, is an important instrument for supporting and promoting good governance. It is assumed that an effective and efficient civil service contributes to the sustenance of good governance. The global dimension of performance management has been rapidly diffused by new management reforms implemented through, and by, multilateral and bilateral mechanisms. A big component of this increasingly global agenda has been the concern by some developed countries to achieve more with less or the same resources. New managerialism often encapsulates the practice of customising the delivery of service by the public servants.

GLOBAL GOVERNANCE AND THE ROLE OF THE STATE

The liberalisation and globalisation process has brought to the fore the question of the role of the state. The question centres around what the state can do when most of its functions are absorbed by the globalisation process and when, equally, some functions have been decentralised, commercialised and even privatised.

In terms of the political economy of structural adjustment, the good governance agenda is also vitally concerned with issues surrounding the role of the state in domestic economic management. This concern relates to the fact that, in many developing countries, the state emerged in the post-war era as the principal agent of economic change, with the result that the state sector came to play a dominant, and in many instances, *the* dominant role in the strategy of economic development. It was reflected, *inter alia*, in pervasive state-ownership of key production and commercial activities, its high contribution to levels of GDP and its deep regulatory presence in the economy.

The new political economy ideology that underpins the linked strategies of structural adjustment and good governance originates from the prior indictment of state involvement in, and management of, the economy as the central obstacles to economic progress. From this perspective, governments are seen as constraining overall national economic performance by assuming tasks, particularly in the area of production, that are best left to the private sector, on the one hand, and by putting into place a host of economic controls and regulations, with distortionary effects and inefficiency consequences, on the other.[9]

The criticism of the state is based on the assumption that it is basically exploitative or predatory, the captive, moreover, of special interest groups, exacting rents for itself and these factional interests, with marginal concern for the public or national good.

The state is under pressure to change both its policy and operational approaches to economic development. The reasons for this pressure for change in the role of the state are:

- it allows the state to concentrate on those activities in which it has decided comparative advantage – in the areas of macro-economic policy-making and the provision of delivery of a range of social, security and legal services and infrastructural development, which together are so crucial to the establishment of an enabling environment for private sector development;

- it opens the way for expanded private sector involvement in productive, commercial and other economic activities – an involvement that is intended to bring with it benefits relating to market competition, efficiency criteria, risk-taking behaviour and the like;

- by getting involved in a narrower and more focused set of tasks, the state is enabled to use more rationally and effectively the limited technical, managerial and professional skills that characterise many of the poorer developing countries, thereby being in a position to improve the management of residual public sector activities.[10]

The reform programme is intended to cater for both the traditional civil service and the public enterprise sector in many Commonwealth countries. Its overall focus is on management capacities of public institutions in the evolving new context of market economics. State enterprises that are not candidates for privatisation thus find themselves having to undertake programmes of managerial, technical and financial overhaul aimed at creating more efficient and effective operating entities. Simultaneously, moreover, comprehensive programmes of civil service reform are now integral parts of structural adjustment programmes under the International Monetary Fund (IMF) sponsorship. The following objectives are the core of such reform efforts:

(i)   the rationalisation, in terms of its size, cost and functions, of overall public sector and specific public enterprises;

(ii)   the introduction of more effective systems of financial accountability;

(iii)   a greater transparency in the operations of these public institutions;

(iv)   the upgrading of the skills base of the sector and the modernisation of its functional principles, procedures and systems;

(v)   the development of a realistic remuneration policy based on performance.

The successful implementation of all these policy measures depends on a number of factors, some of which are the commitment of the leadership, and the enabling environment with which policies are implemented. Appropriate human resources, skills, knowledge and technology and, above all, instruments, processes, procedures and systems can facilitate the translation of policies into action and the delivery of service. Performance appraisal systems are essential instruments that can be used to measure the extent to which the human resources or employees are delivering the required and expected service. Performance management systems are therefore not only at the tail end of promoting good governance but also are at the direct interface with those who receive the service. It is, therefore, incumbent upon the state to formulate the appropriate performance management system which includes needs analysis, implementation and evaluation and, more importantly, to design the relevant performance appraisal instruments. Such instruments should be designed and understood by the people who use them and should be made part of the overall administrative and management processes and procedures. In this regard, the instruments should be transparent and objective, indicating the degree of accountability. Performance appraisal systems are perceived as affecting qualitative and 'value for money' service delivery to citizens. It is one of the ways in which the general public, and ultimately politicians, become aware of the gap between state and citizens, which can become larger and larger unless there is a suitable checking mechanism.

In supporting the legitimacy of good governance, many countries have embarked upon a strategy of performance governance in which the economy, efficiency, effectiveness and quality are the essential criteria for service delivery and policy management. Such a strategy includes three key elements:

1. reducing the share of government of social resources by focusing on key tasks;

2. enhancing performance management in the public sector itself which is about well-performing policy management and service delivery; and

3. putting the role of the state into perspective as networks govern interactions in society and collaborating with other organisations in ensuring that services are delivered efficiently.

The whole performance management debate focuses on:

1. Contract-oriented and results-based steering organisations, operationalised in the use of performance information in the policy and financial cycle.

2. The creation of an autonomous 'periphery' of organisational units which have operational responsibility and are accountable for their performance to central government units (ministries and departments).

3. The use of market-type mechanisms, such as competitive tendering and contracting out.

These crucial characteristics of performance management constitute some of the important aspects of an enabling environment which is conducive to promoting efficiency. The performance management system does not operate in a vacuum but in a culture and philosophy, with resources and needs of the public and social and political environment.

Most of the developing and some developed countries have established performance management systems and there are already comparative analyses available on their experiences of performance budgeting, management, contracting out, decentralised personnel policy, and the transfer of public management theories and practices.

PRODUCTIVITY IMPROVEMENTS

One of the basic pillars of good governance is productivity. Both the public and private sectors are increasingly under pressure from their members to improve productivity. In the private sector, increased productivity results in an increase in profits while in the public sector, it results in a surplus which in turn increases the supply of service in response to increased demand.

Within the public sector, productivity can be defined as the efficient use of resources, for example, labour, capital, land, time, materials, energy and information, in the production of various goods and services. Increased or higher productivity would imply the accomplishment of more with the same amount of resources or achieving higher output in terms of quantity and quality for the same input. It is in this context that the state expects the public administration system to achieve economic growth, sustainable development and good governance.

Efficiency and effectiveness become critical factors in the delivery of services to the public. It is a matter of great concern to both providers and recipients of services that resources be utilised for the purposes for which they were designed. Productivity takes many forms. It should be quantitative or qualitative, in nature, and may also be finance-driven in that it arises out of the need to save money or to reduce public expenditure with the hope that productivity will improve. In the current debate on public service reform, productivity is at the centre of change management. In the New Zealand public sector context, productivity was considered at three levels:

- productivity change for the service as a whole, or for a particular agency;

- productivity change for specific activities within agencies, (e.g. measuring changes only in one or more sectors of the organisation);

The purpose of seeking productivity improvement is to ensure that the stakeholders in the public sector can benefit from value for money and quality services. It also enables government to achieve its objectives and develop its policies and leads to employers receiving recognition and job satisfaction.

Many Commonwealth countries, aware of the need to improve performance in the public service, have established formal centres that are responsible for productivity across the entire civil service.

One of the first productivity programmes undertaken by the Government of Malaysia, for example, was the Productivity Measurement Programme and a Technical Committee was set up to develop the programme. The four main objectives of the Productivity Management Division were:

1. to provide advisory and consultancy services to government agencies with regard to productivity measurement and improvement;

2. to conduct studies on behavioural aspects, work environment etc. which can affect productivity;

3. to monitor and co-ordinate productivity measurement and improvement efforts by government agencies; and

4. to increase the awareness of public sector agencies of the need and importance of productivity measurement and improvement.[12]

In order to facilitate the process of productivity improvement the Malaysian government introduced several administrative measures such as the implementation of Total Quality Management, encouragement of innovations in the public service; introduction of the client's charter; introduction of Performance Indicators; introduction of the modified Budgeting System, Micro-Accounting system, internal audit system and the introduction of the New Performance Appraisal system. Improvements in systems and procedures, office automation and information technology were also introduced.

The government took further measures to strengthen factors which influence productivity and these were human resources development, systems and procedures, organisational structures and management style, work environment, technology, materials and capital equipment.

As can be seen in the Malaysian example on productivity, there was commitment by the leadership first to make the civil service aware of the importance of productivity; secondly to provide the relevant resources with which to implement the productivity policies; thirdly to reorganise the administrative systems and procedures so that they can develop a capacity to address productivity concerns; and fourthly to inculcate organisational and cultural values that can underpin productivity improvement and measurement. In addition, staff have been trained in the measurement of productivity in, for example, the identification of the main output in line with the objective of the organisation; the determination of productivity indicators, data collection and evaluation of current productivity levels.

As a result of these measures, put in place by the government, it has been possible to measure the extent to which resources are utilised; the extent of operational flexibility in the utilisation of human resources and equipment; identification of areas for productivity improvement; and the organisation's operational costs. In all instances, productivity measurements have focused on finance, human resources, materials and technology which are the principal factors of production. Many governments have now established productivity centres as a means of improving performance in the public service. Among those countries that have established such centres are Singapore, Botswana, Tanzania, Ghana, to mention but a few.

PERFORMANCE MEASUREMENT AS A DETERRENT TO CORRUPTION

Good governance issues have become a focal point in the economic and political agenda of most Commonwealth countries. Many strategies to promote and strengthen good governance have been instituted by interested governments. However, good governance has to be identified and measured. Performance management systems, such as performance appraisal and performance benchmarking, have been used not only as instruments to strengthen good governance but also as a means of discouraging corruption. Most countries have recognised that weak capacities, weak governance and poor accountability in public sector institutions and the lack of a transparent and stable regulatory environment conducive to private sector activities, undermine policy reforms, project outcome, macro-economic stability and sustainable growth.

Corruption is one manifestation of weak governance and is a major concern of governments, citizens, NGOs and donors. The increase in corruption throughout the world has in turn led to an increase ways of combatting corruption and improving governance. Many suggestions have been made, arising partly from changing attitudes towards transnational bribery and partly from the effects of information technology in both developed and developing countries. The attempts to deter corruption are based on the assumption that strengthening good governance and control of corruption contribute significantly to sustainable growth and economic and social development.

The causes of poor governance and corruption in any country are relative and situational. They therefore vary from one country to another and are rooted in the country's politics, bureaucratic traditions and social history. Poor governance is a reflection of weak institutions characterised by a lack of public management capacity and the absence of the rule of law. Capacity for public sector management is increasingly seen as a key requirement of sustained economic growth and is underpinned by transparency and accountability.[13]

Corruption, the abuse of public office for private gain, challenges every country despite formal laws. The discretion of many public officials may be open to abuse because of badly-defined, ever-changing, and poorly disseminated rules and regulations. Accountability will suffer if the ethical values of a well-performing bureaucracy are eroded or never built, rules of conduct and conflict of interest are not enforced, financial management system are dilapidated, no formal mechanisms exist to hold public officials accountable for results, and the "watchdog" bodies that should scrutinise government performance (such as ombudsmen and external auditors, the press, civil society) are ineffectual or disorganised. Critical to accountability is transparency of government budgets, financial reports and department and agency activities generally, so that performance is open to scrutiny.

Many international organisations, including the Commonwealth, assist countries to improve governance and control corruption by improving transparency, accountability and the capacity of public institutions. The Commonwealth Secretariat in particular, has designed programmes to enable countries to establish a predictable and transparent framework of rules, procedures and institutions for the conduct of private and public business, primarily by assisting in the areas of policy development and management, public-sector and management principles and practices.

In addition, issue-based and problem-focused policy and management programmes have been mounted in order to support the decision-making processes and management instruments. The provision of advisory and consultancy services and the organisation of short workshops covering such topics as Cabinet support; procurement and negotiations training; political and administrative interface; the relationship between elected and appointed officials; records and information management; ombudsman support programmes for strengthening governance; and strategic planning and management of change, all contribute to the strengthening of the public service as a machinery of government.

In an attempt to deter corruption and improve governance, the Commonwealth advocates a more pro-active approach in advocating policies and the development of institutions systems and instruments that aim to eliminate the opportunities for corruption and fraudulent activities.

Performance management system is one of the instruments considered necessary as a checking mechanism because essentially it contributes to the promotion and maintenance of good governance.

Performance appraisal, as an instrument of measuring performance, is therefore one of the mechanisms for enforcing the maintenance of good governance, efficiency and effectiveness. However, for performance appraisal to be effective and meaningful, it must operate in a conducive policy, economic and political environment. Since, it measures the extent to which objectives, tasks and duties have been executed by public officials for the good of the public, it must itself be equally transparent, objective and open to scrutiny.

THE CHALLENGE TO MANAGERS

In order to enable staff to increase productivity and improve performance, promote and maintain good governance and achieve the desired results, managers face more turbulent times as they negotiate their way through a world of change and desire to produce the results. The managers and organisations have to learn how to operate differently under the pressure of changing circumstances. Managers have realised that traditional approaches to strategies do not work in today's pattern of rapid, unpredictable and all-consuming change.

In industry after industry, yesterday's business models are being supplemented by radical new ways of doing business. The challenge for managers is therefore to design systems and instruments which suit the more modern management practices, designed to address the strategic issues. In responding to the changing environment and adjusting to the increasing demands for better services managers face different types of challenges. The challenges, while not new, vary from situation to situation but are conceptualised within the global changes and expectations. The following are a few of these challenges:

1. ***People make the critical difference between success and failure*** The challenge relates to the effectiveness with which organisations manage, develop, motivate, involve and engage the willing contribution of the people who work for them. It is a key determinant of how well organisations perform. The proper management of people to improve performance therefore becomes critical to managers and employees alike.

2. ***Knowledge management*** As knowledge replaces financial and physical capital as the critical scarce resource, managers are being challenged to create organisational environments that develop, leverage and capitalise on this valuable competitive asset. But creating knowledge will not necessarily generate the desired results. Crucially, it is not just what and how much individuals learn, but how effectively they can transfer their knowledge throughout the organisation and how effectively it can be applied. Knowledge management is, above all, concerned with people or employees and their behaviour. The challenge relates to the way managers link the management of knowledge and organisational learning. We have already discussed how knowledge can be diffused through the globalisation process. There is so much knowledge that can be shared between and among states and international organisations, especially on performance measurement.

3. *Managing Performance* The continuing drive for improved performance requires new ways of managing, different ways of working and a much broader base of knowledge and skills. People are expected to assume much greater responsibility for their own performance and to have the skills and behaviours that enable them to perform effectively. On a daily basis, managers have to consider and review the factors that can contribute to high performance and how to motivate today's managers who are subject to portfolio careers and operate in flatter structures and non-hierarchical environments.

4. *Keeping ahead of the law* New legislation and codes of practices, the latest decisions of courts which impinge on employees and the latest tribunals and rulings from the courts – all these have implications for organisations. Managers have to be aware of the implications that legal changes bring to bear on their organisations and on their employees.

5. *Practitioner updates* With the public service having been restructured, downsized, decentralised etc., the recruitment and selection methods of new staff will have to change to suit new structures. Where promotions and advancement procedures are based on merit instead of seniority only, new instruments have to be designed in order to respond appropriately to new challenges. The same is expected when dealing with stress in the work-place, motivating staff and sometimes disciplining them. Managers have consistently to review their roles in gaining the commitment of their employees to produce and deliver quality results.

6. *Knowledge Management and Organisational Learning* Organisational learning, knowledge-sharing, continuous improvement, team-based rewards, employee empowerment, high levels of customer service and satisfaction and the formation of business partnerships are the key ingredients of future organisational success. These can be done through learning which drives an organisation's ability to adapt and handle change. Creating new knowledge constitutes a competitive advantage. Personnel and development professionals are crucially positioned to influence and develop the channels through which knowledge is acquired, captured and leveraged.

7. *Developing People through Performance Management* In order to ensure the improvement in performance of their staff, managers consistently ask themselves the following questions:

- How do you ensure that performance management supports the business and other human resources practices?

- How do personal development plans and competency frameworks link to performance management?

- What role do managers need to play in ensuring the success of performance management?

These and many more are the questions that managers of human resources have to grapple with in order to improve the performance of individuals. It is argued that both managers and employees have to create an organisation, culture, policy framework and human resource practices conducive to improved performance. Improvement in performance by employees can also be achieved by a well-designed appraisal instrument. The major reasons for having performance appraisal in place are as follows:

1. To ensure that the performance of staff against the objectives is met.

2. To measure the performance of staff against the objectives set with them at the last performance appraisal.

3. To identify the strengths and weaknesses of staff and to prepare a programme that will both build on their strengths and correct their weaknesses.

4. To determine the underlying reasons for strong and weak performance in order to determine the people with potential as future supervisors or managers.

5. To instigate a mutually agreed action plan for development of staff.

6. To create a climate for two-way discussion which will extend to a communication pattern.

7.   To allow staff to offer feed back to you, particularly on ways in which you have helped or hindered them.[14] The benefits of a successful performance appraisal scheme accrue to the organisation, appraiser, appraisee and the customer or client.

Within the public service reforms in Commonwealth countries, the objectives of the performance review and development system have been clearly stated by Noella Jorm as:

Developing the culture of new professionalism in the public sector through:

- linking the tasks of each department and each employee to the key tasks and key results for each agency;

- providing a set of required behaviours aimed at the development of employee skills and behaviours required to achieve "new professionalism";

- providing processes for improved work planning;

- providing processes which clarify authority, responsibility reporting and accountability relationships;

- identifying competence and allow the privatisation of training and development needs of employees;

- provide an opportunity for improved dialogue between managers, supervisors and employees;

- encouraging the early identification and turn around of unsatisfactory performance;

- recognising and rewarding good performance through appreciation and incentive awards and opportunities for career development;

- appraising the performance of all employees in an open, objective, fair and consistent manner.[15]

These activities jointly contribute towards the reconstruction of the performance appraisal in order to suit the new administrative changes and the rising expectation among employees to develop an open transparent evaluation system.

THE DISINTEGRATION OF THE PRE-INDEPENDENCE APPRAISAL SYSTEM

In the public sector, performance appraisals are not new. They were in existence during the colonial era although for different reasons, i.e. supporting the colonial administration. While they were effective and appropriate in the colonial administration, they could not fit the new dispensation following the achievement of political independence. Self-rule ushered in a new set of managers, employees, organisational structures, objectives, needs and demands of the majority of people. The pre-independence administration structures were dominated by expatriates managing small number of ministries and civil servants with limited objectives. In its earliest manifestation within the framework of the colonial polity, the central administration basically existed to serve the pre-eminent colonial interests. More precisely, it had a severely limited mandate, focused primarily on security matters, and the virtually expatriate staffing at the senior administrative levels ensured as much. Its task environment coincided with the pursuit of the overriding interests of the colonial power and in relation to its domestic focus, with safeguarding the socio-economic advantages of the local population. In other words, public administration, such as it existed, was almost completely alienated from the direct day-to-day concerns of the majority colonised population.

The performance appraisal instrument then in place did not allow discourse between the supervisor and supervisee, did not create an environment in which to discuss goal-setting and the appraisal instrument was designed abroad without taking into account the concerns of the local staff.

After independence, the old bureaucratic system began to disintegrate as it could no longer cope with the new administrative changes and expectations. There was a clear recognition of the necessity for an effective administrative capacity to implement the modified functions that were required of the new public service. Moreover, the post-independence state was closely associated with the general ideological tendency towards the re-definition of the state's role in economic development that was at the core of demanding self-rule. The new administration had to be linked with the broad-based societal transformation as dictated by demands for self-rule.

Although there were many reasons for the disintegration of the pre-independence performance management system, the following can be identified.

- Increasingly, the ability of the civil services to carry out critical – much less the routine – functions of government had been found severely deficient. Furthermore, the size and cost of many of the civil services were deemed excessive and thus became targets for reform. However, the major problems of post-independence public administration have been identified as:

  (i)   over-staffing generally, but particularly in the lower grades;
  (ii) serious shortages of appropriate skills;
  (iii) excessive costs in running the bureaucracy;
  (iv) inadequate human resource management;
  (v)   pervasive corruption and lack of accountability.

The rigid and inflexible public administration was no longer capable of spearheading changes as expected by society. The performance appraisal instruments that were used during the colonial era were never modified in many of the countries following independence. They were also found to be ineffective following the administrative reforms of the 1980s and 1990s. The administrative reforms clarified the mission statements, objectives, tasks and functions of ministries. The performance appraisal instruments were therefore meant to measure the extent to which the tasks were to be achieved. Consequently, the performance appraisal was found wanting, giving rise to the need for designing new ones which would be appropriate to the emerging needs.

The inherited colonial performance appraisal system, which had never been reviewed at independence, could not be relevant to the administrative reforms. In the public sector financial management, for example, the Government of Samoa adopted performance budgeting whose principal features were:

- identification of outputs – goods and services provided by a department to its customers;

- definition of the quantity and quality of those outputs as well as their cost;

- full distribution of a department's overheads to its inputs;

- forward estimates, two years ahead of the current year;

- contractual obligation to deliver budgeted outputs through performance agreements applied to departmental heads initially, then to officers at lower levels of management.16

The colonial performance management system was never designed to achieve the above and consequently was incapable of addressing issues of productivity and efficiency in delivering services to the masses.

- ***Records management in shambles*** The Management and Training Services Division of the Commonwealth Secretariat conducted a needs assessment on Records Management. Although the study initially covered only a few countries, it later appeared that many other countries faced exactly the same problem. The study covered the South Pacific (Samoa, Tonga, Solomon Islands, Vanuatu, Fiji and Papua New Guinea); the Caribbean (Grenada, St Kitts and Nevis, St Vincent and the Grenadines, Guyana and Antigua and Barbuda); and Africa (Gambia, Ghana, Zimbabwe and Zambia). As a result of the study, a greater number of requests have been received by the Commonwealth Secretariat for technical assistance in records management. The survey revealed that some of the records management systems had broken down. It was not possible, for example, to retrieve records from the Registry and Archives, the classification system of correspondence was inadequate and most people used their memories to recollect the whereabouts of certain documents. The system was so widespread that if the registry officer was away from the office, nobody could easily locate the file. The method of handling and accounting for mail, files received, actioned and dispatched left much to be desired.17

- ***Political interference*** Soon after independence there was an increased desire by politicians to control public bureaucracy. The increase was generated by a range of considerations:

  (i)   the new, ideological basis of state action;
  (ii) the dramatic expansion in the tasks of governmental agencies;
  (iii) the related factor of extensive institution-building
  (iv) the imperative of tight political surveillance over the public administration to assure authoritarian control;

(v) the fact that the public service at independence was an inherently conservative institution whose dominant leadership was essentially middle class, accustomed to interacting with and accommodating the interests of the other socio-political élite in society.

The public service, in general, was accused of inhibiting vital change and new approaches. It was a service geared towards impeding progress, safety and caution rather than drive and imagination and were the qualities cultivated by the public administration. The resistance to change by the public service has also been experienced in the United Kingdom. Mr Tony Blair, The Prime Minister, for example said that there were some wonderful people with a tremendous commitment to public service, "but you try getting change in the public sector and the public services. I bear scars on my back after two years in government and heaven knows what it will be like after a bit longer. People in the public sector were more rooted to the concept that if it has always been done this way it might always be done this way, than any group of people I have come across."18

In many Third World countries, resistance to change by the public service was a justification for political interference by politicians. One of the most direct kinds of interference has always been in the recruitment, appointment and discipline of a public servant. If politicians have their way, there is a likelihood that they will not follow the rules and procedures for appointments and, more specifically, will recruit people of their own political persuasion. The rules of and behaviours for performance measurement are generally lacking in personnel that are politically appointed to public office.

Political interference in the public administration, therefore, contributed to the decline in the use of performance appraisal instruments and in the decline of the values of integrity, neutrality, objectivity, consistency and confidentiality.

Lack of Leadership Commitment The experiences of many countries shows that heads of departments have long forgotten the use of appraisal for their subordinates. Annual increments, for example, which had been based on positive appraisal were suspended and as a result some of the staff did not see the value of completing the annual confidential report. Further, many staff were not involved in the discussion of their performance. In some cases, they did not even see the completed confidential reports forwarded by the supervisers to the public service commission. The supervisors were not even monitoring the performance

31

management system. The performance appraisal system, therefore, lost the support, credibility and commitment of both the supervisors and the subordinates, thus giving rise to the decline in the importance of the instrument.

Characteristics of Performance Appraisal Instruments In examining the performance appraisal systems in existence in many countries, it has been possible to identify the common characteristics of the instrument. This has been the case, despite independence and changes in governments. The common characteristics are:

- the appraisal measured personality traits such as obedience, loyalty, smartness, etc. and did not measure objectives and core competencies;

- there were no observable or measurable behaviours which could be compared with other subordinates;

- the system could not cope with strategic planning since it was not participative in the sense of involving the subordinates when their appraisals were being conducted;

- the system was therefore not developmental to both the organisation and the individual because it lacked monitoring factors.

Consequently, the system was open to bias and abuse, was demotivating, difficult to compare employees, and time-consuming which resulted in disparity in ratings of staff.

The limitations of the system discussed above are a good cause for developing a new performance appraisal instrument which is bias-free, which allows integrated and strategic planning, is participative and which has a capacity for continuous learning. In essence, it is a competitive system which has a set of skills, knowledge, abilities, behaviour characteristics and can be seen to predict the desired performance. The performance appraisal instrument which bears these characteristics has a potential for success because it is open, participative transparent and amenable to change to suit the changing environment.

THE PRESSURES FOR CHANGE

While an improved performance management system is desirable in the proper use of available resources, it has nonetheless, been triggered by various forces operating in society. The need to improve the performance appraisal instrument is not automatic but is a result of many sources and factors in society that make it imperative for the public service to change. The following are some of the forces that have brought pressure to bear on management to design new performance approaches.

- The consumers of public service are by far the largest critical mass that has demanded that public service be delivered effectively and explicitly. Civil society sometimes demands that the delivery of service to them must improve. The pressure is placed not only on the organisation but also on the individual officers who deliver the goods and services directly. Some consumers are organised around a particular service, such as transport, health, education, etc. Such special interest consumer groups would directly pressurise the individual ministry or department or the front-line officer to ensure that the delivery of service is improved. They, therefore, constitute a loose evaluating team upon whose performance the officer will be measured.

Consumers seek voice and participation not only in decision-making but also in the implementation and evaluation of some of the policies. Consumers work either as individuals or through their own organisations in civil society. In some countries, governments have deliberately adopted management styles and approaches which emphasise results. In Canada, for example, the government introduced the results-based management model. Managing for results means:

(a) good business planning, i.e. deciding how best to achieve results with the available resources. This implies that a department must have the capacity to identify key results commitments, link departmental results to government priorities and explore other alternatives.

(b) continuous learning in order to improve programmes, policies and services through performance measurement, linking costs and results and involving partners and clients.

(c) being responsive and accountable to citizens, parliament and partners. This implies that the department must have the capacity to report and communicate in a balanced way on issues that people care about, to use performance information to engage citizens and partners and finally to implement incentives related to results.

- Among the most vocal and critical pressure groups for improved delivery of service for the public are the politicians or elected officials. In some countries, ministers have complained that the policies that have been formulated by government are not being implemented by public servants. The pressure for better services is even greater in countries where there are many political parties that compete in the delivery of service. The competition is based not only for humanitarian purposes but also for self-interest on the part of the politician so that he or she can be elected again to represent the people. The competition between and among the various interest groups brings pressure to bear on the public servants to perform better and above all to achieve the set targets.

  Advocacy groups, for example, seek protection of human rights for individuals, minorities and other socially deprived groups in society. Such groups have been placing emphasis on the freedom of speech, the media, removal of gender bias, and advocating democratic processes and institutions.

  Political leaders always seek public support and stability. In this, they support all calls for good governance to achieve their goals. In strengthening democracy, they win the support of the electorate which can increase their probability of being elected again or to retain power.

- The private sector is another institution that demands that better services be provided and appraised so that it can generate economic growth which may result in the creation of employment, a goal required and appreciated by government. For the private sector to operate efficiently, it needs a conducive environment in which to operate. Such an environment can only be made possible by an efficient public service whose performance is regularly monitored. The appraisal of one civil servant contributes to the efficient functioning of the civil service which, in turn, is instrumental towards the creation of a conducive environment.

- Donor community and non-government organisations often demand that their aid be used effectively. Public service is the instrument that delivers aid to the people on behalf of government. Some donors have complained that their aid is not reaching the targeted group. In some countries, donors and non-government organisations have put pressure on governments to change the rules and regulations that impede the successful delivery of services. The reform of the public service has, in some instances, included change in the rules of delivery and change in the way in which public servants are appraised.

Donor agencies would want good management and a good climate for investment because, without this, sound economic policies would not be implemented, broad development goals would not be met and individual aid projects would fail. Good public sector management requires the support of all parts of government with no unfair interference from politicians, police, judiciary or others.

As a result of these pressures and demands for measuring performance, many countries are seeking technical assistance to help them design their own performance appraisal instruments to suit their own unique circumstances. The designing of appraisal instruments requires technical skill, knowledge and competence in needs assessment, training, installation and implementation. This publication takes the reader through the necessary stages and processes of designing the instrument. The country case studies that are provided indicate the complexity of designing and installing the instrument. They also relate to the movements for change emanating from both external and internal forces.

Experience has shown that some countries, working under pressure from unions or staff associations, have quickly rushed to introduce pay-related performance. This has often occurred without going through the stages of having performance agreements, needs analysis and the designing of the performance appraisal instrument itself. In some cases, pay rewards were approved without performance agreements. In such cases, some staff associations and unions become reluctant to discuss performance agreements and appraisals later. Our view is that the steps outlined in this publication should be followed in order to avoid resistance from staff associations. A rush towards pay awards without following the necessary steps can often lead to long drawn out industrial action by the staff associations.

PERFORMANCE MANAGEMENT: ENDS OR MEANS

The approach to designing the instrument and the training of the human resources that utilise it, as advocated in this publication, is based on the following assumptions:

1. It is tailor-made to suit the needs and unique situations of the supervisors, supervised, the nature and type of the organisation and, more importantly, the socio-political and economic development of the country which reflects the level of literacy, skills, technology and culture of the people.

2. It is based on the principle of participation of stakeholders. The involvement process of stakeholders begins from problem identification, conceptualisation of issues, design, implementation and evaluation of the system. The commitment to design and the capacity to transform the system, when it is desirable, depends very much on the extent to which stakeholders have been involved in the process of change.

3. Once designed through the above processes, the instrument secures ownership by the people who use it. Ownership helps the stakeholders to adjust the instrument in order to suit the changing circumstances of the organisation.

4. The design of the performance management system should be regarded as a process and not as an event. As a process it can be adapted to suit requirements of the organisation. As an event, it is tied to time, place and individual persons and is therefore not adjustable.

5. The nature and type of management problem to be resolved is generally understood by the stakeholders before action is taken. The basis for solution of the problem is, therefore, understood by all, even if some may not agree on the timing and target.

6. It is gender-sensitive in that it has a capacity to depict some of the cultural habits, prejudices and attitudes which may prevail in a male-dominated society.

EFFECTIVE AND MEANINGFUL PERFORMANCE MEASUREMENT

In an attempt to design an effective and meaningful performance measurement, experience within the Commonwealth has shown that there are certain stages and steps that have to be taken into account. The steps, which are related and inter-linked to the assumptions discussed above, do not necessarily follow the same sequence wherever the need is identified.

The following steps and questions have been found to be useful in the design of the instrument:

1. A review of the goals and objectives of the organisation and the diagnostic evaluation of the practices, procedures, structures and systems would have to be conducted in order to determine the areas to be measured. The identified areas will assist in determining the methodology, the tools, time and resources to be used in the selection of the performance indicators.

2. In selecting performance indicators, which are appropriate to the objectives and goals of the organisation, it is possible to decide on the kinds of performance measures that best apply to the situation. As discussed above, the process of designing must include the contributions of employees and other stakeholders. At this stage, it is necessary to assess the relevance of the performance measures, which have to be changed in order to achieve what is desirable.

3. Overcoming barriers to implementing performance measures. When any change process is being introduced, it is possible that there are some people who will benefit and that there are equally others who stand to lose. In designing the instrument, therefore, it is advisable to assess the pitfalls and to minimise the risks and barriers to performance measurement. In attempting to overcome some of the barriers, it is necessary to establish a system of measurement which aligns personal performance to organisation's initiatives in order to see their contribution to the goals that have been agreed upon.

The system that is being developed should be flexible and must be related to the public service reforms.

4. Benchmarking is a tool that is often used in developing a performance measurement system. The first step to take, in this regard, is to identify the areas that have to be compared with other similar services and organisations. The process of benchmarking involves the co-operation of people in other organisations to supply the appropriate information required for comparison. This is necessary in order to ensure that one compares like with like in order to achieve the desired results.

5. The will and commitment, particularly of the leadership, in developing a performance measurement, can be achieved through their participation in the identification and solution of the problem. While participation ensures a sense of ownership by the users of the instrument, it is also a way of winning support for the amount of effort it will take to design performance measurement. Indirectly, the involvement process should be able to persuade employees that performance measurement is a way of solving some of the management and organisational problems before they reach the customers and the public.

6. In many organisations, and in particular government ministries and departments, there are officials who are either reluctant to use the system or who have faith in its application. There are equally others who regard it as extra work. These groups of people need to be encouraged to fully understand the advantages of improving the system. Most employees are very suspicious of the use of new instruments. The suspicion may be based on how the results will be used. In many of the countries visited by the authors while collecting data for this publication, it was found that many staff associations or public service unions were reluctant to participate in improving the performance appraisal instrument. This reluctance was based on the fear that the instrument would be used to terminate the employment of many of their colleagues who may be identified as poor performers. Resistance to the introduction of the instrument is regarded as a protection for their members.

7. The relationship between performance measurement and other public service reform initiatives should be clearly explained so that the overall objective of

the measurement is not isolated and lost or treated as novel to the organisation. The linkages can be achieved through communicating to employees that performance measurement is part of a larger quality drive and cannot be seen as an end in itself. The managers would need to devise some ways of ensuring that measurement is related to both the administrative system and to human resources. The employees too, should be able to use performance measurement as a way to achieve larger quality goals and objectives of the organisation.

8.   One of the questions often asked following the designing of the instrument is how to institutionalise it in the organisation so that it becomes part of the organisational culture. This can be done by managers providing adequate information and communication in order to ensure that people do not interpret performance measurement as lack of confidence in their work. Employees who, in turn, can explain such benefits to their colleagues in the work-place should appreciate the benefits of performance measurement.

9.   When the performance measurement has been designed, managers need to use the result to drive a continuous change within the organisation. This can be done through continually re-assessing performance aims in relation to the changes in the goals and objectives of the organisation. The data in the organisation should be interpreted periodically in order to determine areas that need improvement and decide on the best way of using the findings to drive further change, for example, improving the delivery of service to the public. The whole process of transition needs to be closely monitored to ensure consistency and continuity by demonstrating the tangible results of the initiative.

CONCLUSION

The need to develop a performance management system in the public service can be regarded both as means to an end and as an end in itself. It is a means to an end in that it is a contributory factor to the solutions of some of the management problems and it also facilitates the change process in policy and management systems and structures. Public service reform, for example, has resulted in the need to restructure or to downsize or right-size, to review the management principles of delegation and or decentralisation, to develop strategic plans, review accounting procedures, change policy measures, respond to the demand by the citizens for improved delivery of service, control, staff guidance and development, the review of standards of discipline, recruitment, promotion and the training of human resources. All these management practices require that a system be developed which can demonstrate that the goals of the organisation are being achieved. In this regard, it is an important instrument in assessing the strengths and weaknesses of the organisation, human resources, procedures and practices, and systems and structures.

Further, it is an instrument in that it can be used as a basis for developing the legal framework, which justifies and authorises the use of the instrument in the public service. The Public Service Act and the Administrative Circulars are some of the legal and administrative instruments that are used to back up the installation of performance measurement into the public service machinery. Finally, and more importantly, it helps to link pay or rewards to the performance of human resources.

The performance management system is an end in itself because top management feels sensitised to the core activities and contents of the system. Because both employers and employees are involved in the development of the performance management system, they develop an understanding of the requisite skills, knowledge and attitudes. Together, stakeholders constitute a conducive environment in which the performance management system is not only developed but also institutionalised. The performance management instrument therefore, finds its home within the total management structures of the administrative system and can be a critical catalyst in the reform of the public service as an instrument of the state. Since it is part of the home, there is a general feeling among the stakeholders that the performance management instrument, once designed, belongs to them and can be changed by them.

REFERENCES

1. Side by Side: The New Performance Agreements Manual by John Sullivan and Frank Spencer Vitascope Productions, Melbourne, Australia 1992.

2. Canadian Centre for Development: Continuous Learning. A CCMD Report No. 1, May 1994, Canada.

3. Korac-Kakabadse, A and Korac-Kakabadse N, Leadership in Government: Study of the Australian Public Service. Ashgate, Aldershop, England 1998. p 135.

4. Thomas, V., Globalisation: implications for development learning: Public Administration and Development. The International Journal of Management Research and Practice. CAPAM and John Siley & Sons Ltd. Vol 19 No. 1, February 1999.

5. Commonwealth Secretariat: Information Technology Policies and Applications in the Commonwealth Developing countries: Mayuri Odedra and Shirin Madon – edited by G. Harindramath and Jonathan Liebenau 1993 p 12 in Okut-Uma, R. W. 'O., Information technology policy initiatives revisited: a Commonwealth case study analysis; Information Technology Policies, proceedings of the workshop held at Beaumont College, UK (November 1990) 1991.

6. Panchamukhi, V. R., Globalisation, Competition and Economic Stability: Paradigm Vol. 1 No. 2, January 1998 (14-31).

7. Summary: UN Human Development Report 1999 p 1.

8. Buse, K., Globalisation and the Changing Roles of International Health Organisations. Health in the Commonwealth: Challenges and Solutions 1998/99. Produced by Kingston Publications Ltd. for the Commonwealth Secretariat.

9. Ferguson, Tyrone, Structural Adjustment and Good Governance: The case of Guyana, Public Affairs Consulting Enterprise, Guyana, 1995 p 16.

10. op cit p 166.

11. Commonwealth Secretariat: Current Good Practices and New Developments in Public Service Management: A Profile of the Public Service of New Zealand. The Public Service Country Profile Series No.5, p. 55.

12. Commonwealth Secretariat: Current Good Practices and New Developments in Public Service Management. A Profile of the Public Service of Malaysia. The Public Service Country Profile Series: No. 3, p 54.

13. World Bank, Discussion Paper: Helping Countries Combat Corruption and Improve Governance, September 8, 1997, p 2.

14. Stan Barnett and John Sullivan: Face to Face. The New Performance Appraisal: Workbook for Video 1, 1992. Vitascope Publications, Australia.

15. Objectives of the Barbados Public Sector Reform Programmes, study by Noella Jorm, independent consultant.

16. Government of Samoa: Statement of Economic Strategy (SES) Treasury Department, Planning and Policy Division, Apia, Samoa, January 1996.

17. Agere, S., Lemieux, V., Mazikana, P., Better Information Practices: Improving Records and Information Management in the Public Service. Commonwealth Secretariat, London, 1999, p 5.

18. UK Prime Minister, Tony Blair, The Times, Wednesday, July 7, 1999.

Figure I

HIERARCHICAL VS DEVELOPMENTAL FEEDBACK

The Hierarchical (Traditional) Feedback Model

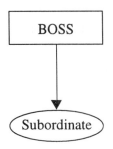

The Developmental (360°) Feedback Model

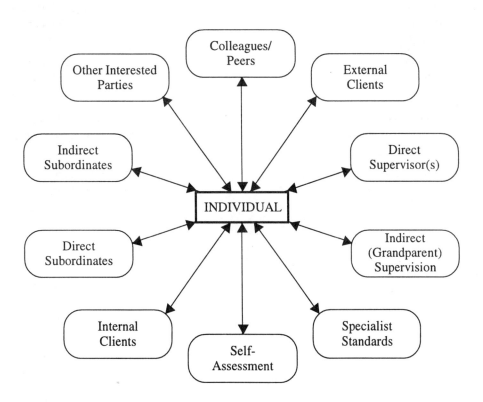

Source: Roger Fernando, Critical Skills Development (CSD), UK

Figure II

THE PERFORMANCE MANAGEMENT CYCLE

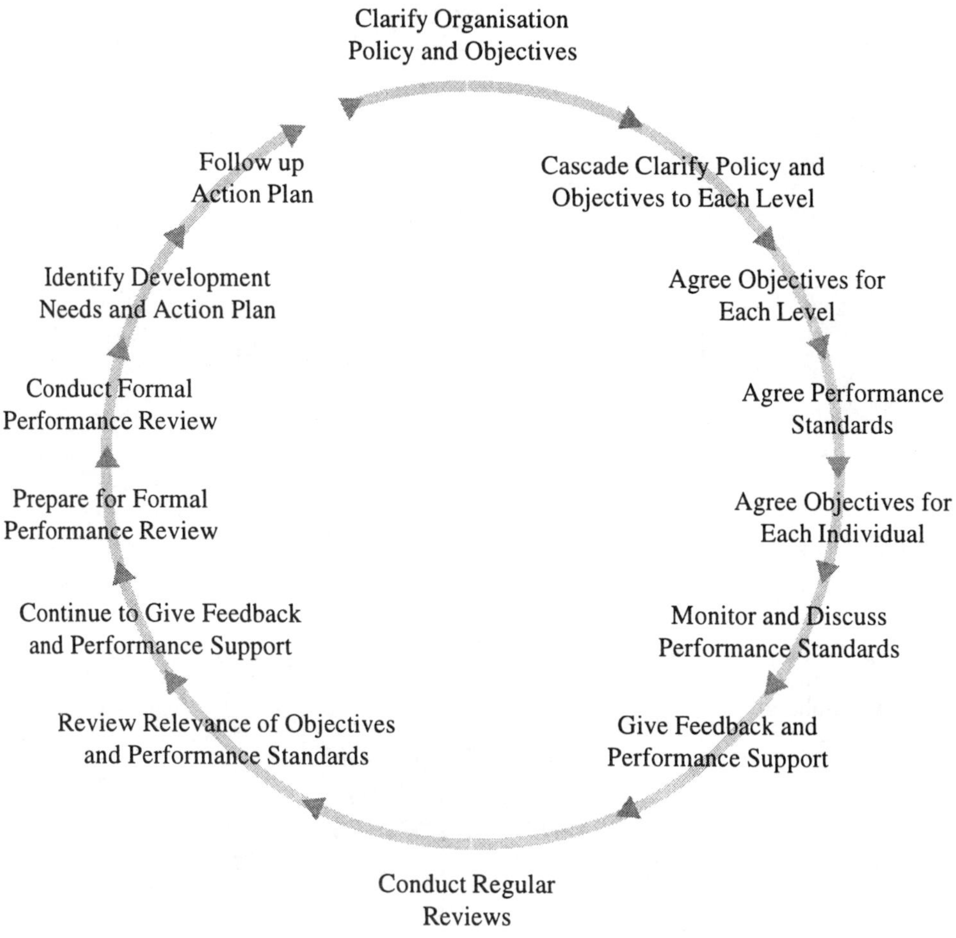

Clarify Organisation
Policy and Objectives

Follow up
Action Plan

Cascade Clarify Policy and
Objectives to Each Level

Identify Development
Needs and Action Plan

Agree Objectives for
Each Level

Conduct Formal
Performance Review

Agree Performance
Standards

Prepare for Formal
Performance Review

Agree Objectives for
Each Individual

Continue to Give Feedback
and Performance Support

Monitor and Discuss
Performance Standards

Review Relevance of Objectives
and Performance Standards

Give Feedback and
Performance Support

Conduct Regular
Reviews

Source: Roger Fernando, Critical Skills Development (CSD), UK

Figure III

Ref:	COMPONENT	ELEMENTS	NOTES
			Applied to:
A.	Performance Indicators	Total 12 Elements	
		Setting Targets and Standards (QQT)	Everyone
		Preparation and Planning	Everyone
		Organisation & Monitoring	Everyone
		Implementation & Getting Results	Everyone
		Problem-Solving & Decision-Making	Everyone
		Managing Information	Everyone
		Managing Relationships	Everyone
		Teamwork (Local and Wider)	Everyone
		Developing Subordinate(s)	Those with subordinates
		Self-Development	Everyone
		Reviewing and Follow-Up	Everyone
		Constructive Development and Innovation	Everyone
B.	Performance Standards	(Total 6 Elements)	Meaning of Element
		Unacceptable	Failing to meet most objectives/targets or requirements of the work and demonstrating a lack of commitment to performance improvement, or demonstrating a lack of ability to improve.
		Basic	Only just meeting the most basic standards of the work, although a number of factors of the objective/target have not been met. There is clearly room for improvement in several specific areas.

45

Developing	Achievement stronger in some aspects of the work than in others. Most factors of the objective/target met, but performance falls short of full achievement. There is clear evidence of commitment to improvement.
Fully Achieved	Fully achieves, or has few, if any failures in meeting all required objectives/targets of the work and meets all normal job requirements.
Very Effective/Exceeding Expectations	Some agreed targets constructively exceeded. All other targets fully achieved. Thorough, proficient and highly committed beyond normal expectations.
Exceptional/Excellent	Most agreed targets consistently exceeded constructively. All other targets fully achieved. Very exceptional, highly professional, dedicated and excellent contribution well beyond normal expectations.

Source: Roger Fernando, Critical Skills Development (CSD) UK

NEEDS ASSESSMENT

BACKGROUND

Organisational reform during the past two decades has commonly involved a number of actions. These include devolution of responsibility for managing people to departments, and central agencies adopting budgetary, strategic planning, policy development, information provision, and programme and policy monitoring roles.

Central agencies have been involved in the development of government vision and mission statements, goals and performance measures and flow-down key result areas and measures for government departments. Central agencies have also initiated and supported the introduction of programme budgeting and contract employment for senior managers. Regulatory and policy development has included the reform of employment legislation to include concepts such as merit recruitment and selection, employment equity, management and employee ethics and performance-based progression and reward.

Departments have undertaken major internal restructures, often using process-mapping to improve efficiency and redefine job roles and responsibilities. These activities have highlighted the need to reconsider the role of each employee, how well their job is described, understood, performed and rewarded. Records management, job classification, positions description development and the scrutiny of appraisal instrument projects have been a priority.

Best practice performance management has been found to be an ideal catalyst for change during organisational reform. It provides processes and outcomes that bring together and provide synergistic and interdependent relationships between all the key elements of managing people.

THE PERFORMANCE MANAGEMENT SYSTEM

ANALYSING THE ENVIRONMENT

A first step in the consideration of new performance management approaches is the analysis of the total environment in which the organisation is operating.

Consideration should be given to the nature of the political, regulatory, economic, structural, policy and cultural environment. Key questions to be asked include:

- What is the level of government and senior management commitment to modernisation, reform or on-going development of the public sector?

- What time-frame for change is appropriate?

- What changes have already happened?

- What changes are planned?

- Are adequate resources available to develop and implement new performance management approaches?

Performance management approaches can be powerful tools for the strengthening of the public sector. Depending on the circumstances and time-frame for change they can include:

1. developing awareness and understanding of performance management ahead of full performance system reform;

2. adjustment of existing approaches to planning and appraisal to achieve a more integrated performance management approach;

3. introduction of a new performance management approach as a major tool for organisational reform.

EVALUATING THE STATUS OF THE CURRENT PERFORMANCE SYSTEM

Once environmental analysis has provided an overview, the next step in assessing needs for performance management is to evaluate the status of the current performance management approach.

Evaluation of the current system can be undertaken through the conduct of interviews/workshops and focus groups with senior managers, human resources specialists and employees in central agencies and departments. Key questions to be asked include:

- Is there a performance management system?

- Is it standard across government?

- Is there a policy document describing the planning and appraisal processes?

- Is there a standard appraisal form?

- Does the system cover all employees?

- Does it include planning and appraisal processes?

- What percentage of departments has strategic plans?

- What percentage of staff receives appraisals?

- How often does performance planning occur?

- How often do appraisals occur?

- Are the appraisals considered fair?

- Are managers and employees satisfied with the current performance management system?

- What changes would managers and employees like to see in the performance management approach?

Two additional tools are provided below to help you evaluate your organisation's current performance management approach. They are designed to allow performance system weaknesses to be detected and views formed as to whether the system requires strengthening in critical areas or full redesign.

The first of these is a **SWOT** analysis to help identify strengths and weaknesses of the current performance approach and opportunities and threats that may impact on any changes.

The second is a **Diagnostic Survey** that takes into account identified areas of common weakness in performance management approaches. These are Lack of Sponsorship, Lack of Fit to the Culture, Lack of Integration with other Human Resources Processes, Lack of Adequate Measurement of Performance, Lack of Policy Support for the Performance System and Lack of Confidence in Appraisal Judgements.

Completing this survey will help define where major problems exist and provide focus areas for redesign.

Undertake a SWOT analysis to ascertain the strengths & weaknesses of the current performance approach and future opportunities and threats.

Strengths	Weaknesses
What do you believe to be the strengths of your current performance approach?	What are the weaknesses?
e.g. *People are used to the current approach*	e.g. *No links to corporate goals* *Appraisals not conducted regularly*
	Can a weakness be converted to a strength? How?

Threats	Opportunities
What factors in your environment may impact on any changes?	What opportunities exist in the environment for improving your performance approach?
e.g. *Strategic planning is not carried out*	e.g. *Government wants public sector reform*
	Performance contracts and performance pay have been introduced and require a more reliable instrument for assessing performance
Can a threat become an opportunity? How?	

Performance Management System – Key Problem Areas

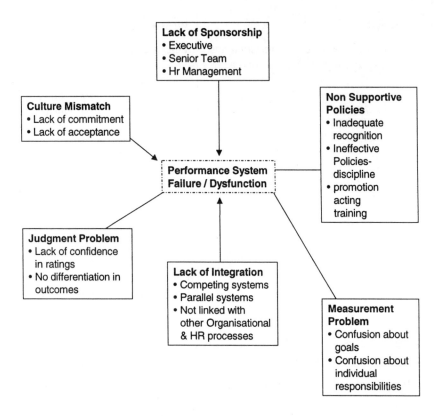

Complete the Diagnostic Survey and Score Sheet to identify problem areas and strategy areas to focus on in system redesign.

Diagnostic Survey – Performance Management System – Key Problem Areas

Tick the appropriate box for each question below.

Sponsorship	Yes	No	NA
1. Does the Executive sign off key performance management communication documents?	☐	☐	☐
2. Does the CEO appraise the performance of the team through a performance management approach?	☐	☐	☐
3. Is data from performance system outcomes reported to the Executive?	☐	☐	☐
4. Are roles and responsibilities in relation to on-going maintenance, development and evaluation of the system clearly defined?	☐	☐	☐

Culture	Yes	No	NA
1. Do employees find the system easy to use and understand?	☐	☐	☐
2. Does the system have clearly defined and known objectives?	☐	☐	☐
3. Do system objectives include culture change and appropriate strategies if this is an objective?	☐	☐	☐
4. Have employees received training in the performance management processes?	☐	☐	☐
5. Do managers regard the system as a useful tool?	☐	☐	☐

Integration	Yes	No	NA
1. Are unit and individual objectives linked to the overall objectives of the organisation?	☐	☐	☐
2. Is the system linked to performance reward initiatives?	☐	☐	☐
3. Are training plans drawn from the performance system?	☐	☐	☐
4. Is the system linked to probation, promotion, performance improvement and discipline systems?	☐	☐	☐
5. Is the system aligned to any quality process system initiatives?	☐	☐	☐
6. Is the system linked to any benchmarking initiatives?	☐	☐	☐

Measurement	Yes	No	NA
1. Is there a clear statement of organisational objectives?	☐	☐	☐
2. Are business unit plans and objectives developed?	☐	☐	☐
3. Do individuals have up-to-date job descriptions?	☐	☐	☐
4. Have employees received training in developing objectives and measures?	☐	☐	☐
5. Are job responsibility boundaries clear?	☐	☐	☐
6. Are generic objectives and measures agreed where a number of employees perform the same function?	☐	☐	☐

Policy	Yes	No	NA
1. Do employees value available reward and recognition strategies?	☐	☐	☐
2. Can adequate sanctions be imposed for poor performance?	☐	☐	☐
3. Do managers' performance agreements include full participation in performance management processes?	☐	☐	☐

Judgement	Yes	No	NA
1. Are appraisal decision judgement processes transparent in the system documents?	☐	☐	☐
2. Have managers received training in giving feedback?	☐	☐	☐
3. Have managers been trained to be aware of bias in making judgements?	☐	☐	☐
4. Can the employee request the input of a next level manager in the performance management processes?	☐	☐	☐

Diagnostic Survey – Score Sheet

Complete number of **No** responses in each area from your survey. A large number, of **No** responses indicates problem areas for your performance management system and focus areas in redesign.

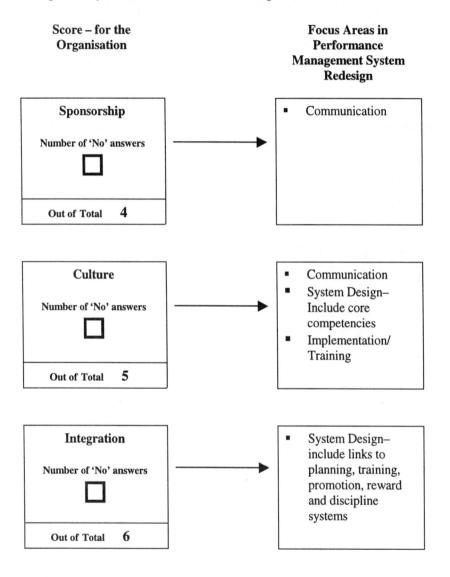

Score – for the Organisation	**Focus Areas in Performance Management System Redesign**

Sponsorship

Number of 'No' answers

☐

Out of Total   **4**

- Communication

Culture

Number of 'No' answers

☐

Out of Total   **5**

- Communication
- System Design– Include core competencies
- Implementation/ Training

Integration

Number of 'No' answers

☐

Out of Total   **6**

- System Design– include links to planning, training, promotion, reward and discipline systems

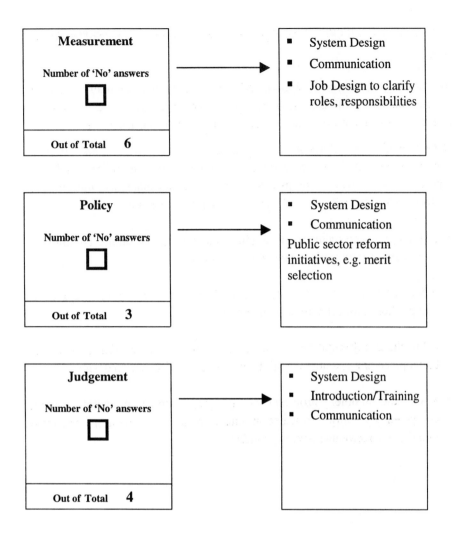

Measurement	
Measurement	• System Design
Number of 'No' answers	• Communication
☐	• Job Design to clarify roles, responsibilities
Out of Total 6	

Policy	• System Design
Number of 'No' answers	• Communication
☐	Public sector reform initiatives, e.g. merit selection
Out of Total 3	

Judgement	• System Design
Number of 'No' answers	• Introduction/Training
☐	• Communication
Out of Total 4	

CONSTRAINTS AND PRESCRIBED REQUIREMENTS FOR A NEW PERFORMANCE SYSTEM

In assessing needs for Performance Management, this document has so far detailed analysis of the environment in which performance management operates and evaluation of the status of the current performance system.

Before considering Performance Management best practice and moving to designing new performance processes, a final step in assessing needs is to consider any constraints or prescribed requirements that may impact on the performance system re-design. The key questions to ask are:

- Has the government or the public sector made any public commitments regarding performance management approaches?

- Are there statements describing new performance management approaches in public sector reform plans and documents?

- Are there any regulations, policies or employee organisation agreements that place any possible constraints on performance system design?

- Are there other programmes, e.g. programme budgeting, quality, competency being introduced that need to be aligned with or incorporated into the performance system design?

Use the template below to help detail how existing constraints/prescriptions can be dealt with:

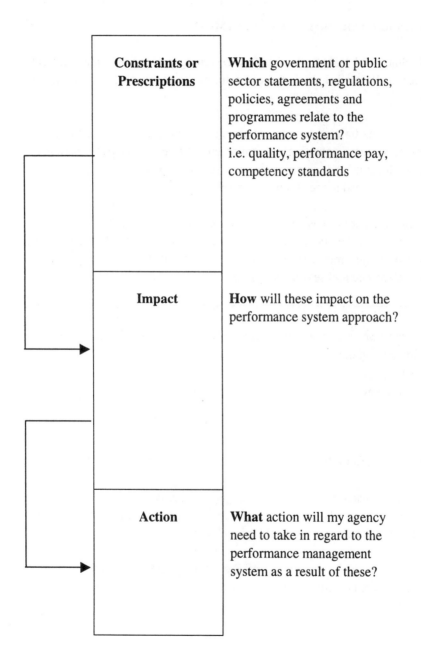

Constraints or Prescriptions	**Which** government or public sector statements, regulations, policies, agreements and programmes relate to the performance system? i.e. quality, performance pay, competency standards
Impact	**How** will these impact on the performance system approach?
Action	**What** action will my agency need to take in regard to the performance management system as a result of these?

DESIGNING THE SYSTEM

UNDERSTANDING PERFORMANCE MANAGEMENT

For individuals and teams modifying or designing performance management approaches, a thorough knowledge of performance management principles is essential.

Resources include training courses, textbooks, articles, details of performance management systems operating in similar environments and participation in workshops, forums and common interest groups. A list of recommended references is provided at the end of section 8.

The system designer needs to remember that while best practice principles represent an ideal, the successful system, while moving towards the ideal, is developed by taking into account local conditions, local acceptability and the objectives identified and set for the system.

> *"Many appraisal systems have failed simply because staff people responsible for planning the system have become engrossed in trying to achieve technical perfection."*
> Randall, G & Fowler, A, Employee Appraisal, 1994

CONSIDERING PERFORMANCE DEVELOPMENT AND SYSTEM TYPES

Performance Management Best Practice is constantly evolving in line with organisational theory. Performance Management brings together work study, planning and measurement and motivational theory.

The table below gives an outline of the developments that led to modern performance management approaches.

Work-Centred, Measurement Approaches	**Person-Centred, Skills Development Approaches**
American Emphasis	**British Emphasis**
F. W. Taylor, scientific management, work measurement, time and motion study, work study, 1910–1950	Personality trait-based approaches, common 1900–1950
	Critique of trait approaches as devaluing individual, 1960s
Measurable results-oriented approaches, Management by Objectives (MBO), 1970s, 1980s	Move to skills development approaches, 1960s

Valuing Work and People

- Quality circles, process standards, motivation through involvement, teams, 1970s onwards;

- Performance Management, incorporates results focus, assessment based on measurable achievements and productivity improvement through skill development, quality and competency approaches, late 1980s, 1990s

The progression of theoretical thinking relating to planning, performance, measurement and development led to the use of appraisal instruments as we know them today. An outline of appraisal instrument types and their strengths and weaknesses is provided in the following table.

Performance System Types

rating on personality
traits –merit rating –
graphic rating scales
 highly open to bias,
demotivating

pen picture difficult to compare
employees

critical incident – narrative time consuming – open
to recency effects/bias

Behaviourally anchored
rating scales (BARS)
behavioural observation
scales (BOS)
 Costly, difficult to
develop

rating on objectives
achieved
 short-term
objectives at
expense of long-
term benefits

performance
management
appraisal
 links objectives of
individual to
objectives of agency

competency-based requires
demonstration of
outputs, can be too
complex and inflexible

performance
management and
core competencies
 current trends favour

Performance management best practice is seen to be defined by a number of factors. These include research data, system design preferences for new systems and quality award criteria.

Research

"Companies with performance management have higher profits, better cash flows, stronger stock market performance than companies without.

Results showed that the following program features are associated with highly effective performance management programs:

- Senior management taking a visible and prominent role in program design and implementation;

- Giving managers common performance measures;

- Emphasizing coaching and feedback; and

- Tailoring implementation methods to fit each company's needs."

Survey Hewitt Associates/Boston Consulting Group/ Holt Financial, 1994.

"85% of organizations surveyed believed that adopting a Performance Management approach improved organizational effectiveness."

Survey UK Institute of Personnel Management, 1991.

System Preferences

"Commonest type of appraisal systems used in Australia are results based"

> *Surveys by Commonwealth Dept of Employment, Deloitte, Haskins & Selles, CCH Australia Ltd. & Australian Graduate School of Management. Reported in Robert Clark – Australian HR Management 1995.*

"72 % of appraisal systems in organizations surveyed had emphasis on future outcomes."

> *Survey of 20 leading Australian companies – Tranter R., Kelly P & Chaffey,1997.*

"Commonwealth Public Service proposes performance management as compulsory legal requirement."

> *Public Service Bill, 1997.*

Quality Award Criteria

"Performance Management – examination of the processes in place to ensure that employees know their roles, contribute to the development of their roles and goals and can obtain timely and effective feedback on their performance."

> *Australian Quality Awards for Business Excellence, 1998*

PUTTING IT ALL TOGETHER – A FLEXIBLE, BEST PRACTICE PERFORMANCE MANAGEMENT MODEL

A decade of experience in monitoring and developing performance management approaches has led to the development of the following best practice performance model.

As discussed earlier, 'best practice' represents an ideal at a particular point in time. While this model is used as a guide in developing the organisation's performance approach, the chosen approach should be firmly grounded in analysing needs. Performance management processes need to suit the total operating environment and needs of the organisation and to be focused on the outcomes desired from performance management.

**Performance Management:
Linking Planning and Management**

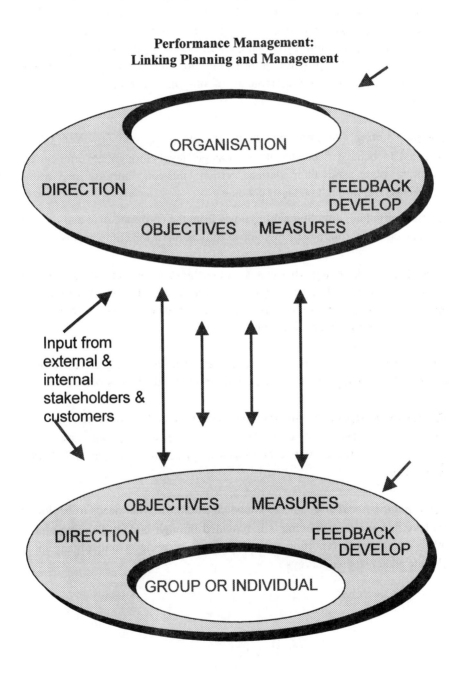

This model describes the performance management system as linking the performance of individuals to the overall direction of the organisation through processes that facilitate the achievement of desired goals.

These processes of direction-setting, objective and target measure development, provision of feedback and the development of additional capabilities are linked, and occur at corporate, strategic, group and individual levels of the organisation. Environmental activities, including stakeholder and customer feedback, provide information for the development of new capabilities to meet the requirements of on-going direction and objective-setting.

Direction-setting –or knowing where you are going and how you will be expected to behave – occurs at the strategic level through government and corporate plans and their defined vision, mission, purpose and values statements, and through codes of conduct.

For the individual, direction-setting flows from the corporate plan and the code of conduct, and through their own job specification or job competencies.

Objectives – or knowing what you want to achieve – are often initially devised and expressed through the strategic result areas of government structural plans and flow down as key result areas, objectives, goals and strategies in corporate plans and departmental business plans.

For the individual, objectives appear as key result areas, objectives or goals, expressed in group plans, job descriptions and individual work plans.

Performance Measures –or knowing how you will know when you have achieved – are expressed as performance measures, indicators, standards or targets in structural, corporate and business plans and in group or individual work plans.

Performance Feedback – or the knowledge to know what needs to be done to achieve or keep on achieving – is provided through budget planning reports, other management reporting systems, capability reviews and organisational climate and customer surveys.

The individual receives and provides feedback through the performance management progress reviews, annual review, 360 degree or other performance feedback schemes, recognition and reward outcomes, and performance improvement plans.

Performance Development is built into the Performance Management model through performance feedback data which informs the organisation of the capacity building and skill development that needs to occur at organisation and individual levels if public sector and government goals are to be met.

DEVELOPING PERFORMANCE MANAGEMENT SYSTEM OBJECTIVES

Once needs have been assessed, constraints and prescriptions identified and performance management approaches and best practice understood, any performance management change needs to be informed by the development of specific objectives for the new or modified performance management system.

The key questions to ask are:

- What performance management change focus has the environmental analysis and assessment of needs, including the SWOT analysis and Diagnostic Survey, indicated?

- What does the government and public want to achieve from its performance management approach?

Example Objective

Developed by an agency wishing to use the new performance system as a culture change tool.

The Performance Review and Development System has been designed to develop a culture of 'new professionalism' in the public sector through:

- linking the tasks of each department and each employee to the key tasks and key results for each agency;

- providing a set of required behaviours aimed at the development of employee skills and behaviours required to achieve "new professionalism";

- providing processes for improved work planning;

- providing processes which clarify authority, responsibility, reporting and accountability relationships;

- identifying competence and prioritizing training and development needs of employees;

- providing an opportunity for improved dialogue between managers, supervisors and employees;

- encouraging the early identification and turnaround of unsatisfactory performance;

- recognising and rewarding good performance through appreciation, incentive awards and opportunities for career development;

- appraising the performance of all employees in an open objective, fair and consistent manner.

Example drawn from the Government of Barbados

SELECTING COMPONENTS FOR THE NEW SYSTEMS

The selection of components for the modified or new performance system will be based on the needs assessment and other research undertaken, including the consideration of best practice. The system objectives will reflect these and provide a guide for your system design.

The components to be included in the performance management system will include policies, processes and documents.

Policies

A performance management policy is generally formulated to set the rules for the performance approach. The development of this policy will set boundaries for the system and ensure appropriate integration with other systems. It will also establish the level of compliance required.

Key questions to be considered in developing performance management policy include:

- Who will be covered by the performance management system?

- Will senior management and heads of department be included in the system?

- Will employees be appraised on behaviours demonstrated and objectives achieved, or just on objectives?

- What will be the implications of appraisal?

- How will appraisal impact on career development, promotion, pay and other reward and recognition systems and discipline systems?

- How will consideration of equity issues be incorporated?

- What will be the confidentiality requirements?

Processes

Performance management processes govern the flow and timings of information and actions relating to the performance management system. Key questions to ask include:

- Will individuals all develop objectives and be appraised at one time of the year?

- How will the strategic planning cycle be linked to the individual performance cycle?

- How will training to obtain on-going performance improvement be linked?

- How and where will performance documents be stored, both during the appraisal year and in the longer term?

- What grievance processes will be included in the performance management system?
- How will performance results be linked to reward, recognition and discipline processes?

DOCUMENTS

Key performance management documents generally include the performance management policy document, which is part of the organisation's policy manual, a user guide for each employee and an annual appraisal form. Key questions to consider when preparing the user guide and form are:

- Are the documents easy to use and understand?

- Can each document 'stand alone' i.e. if the user guide is lost; will the appraisal form guide users through the required processes?

- Have the forms been tested with employees to ensure that they are easy to use and understand?

A Best Practice Checklist for Performance Management System Components

"A sound Performance Management system will encourage the use of reasoned, unbiased judgement and provide the transparency to make it evident when this is not occurring."

Transparency
- include objectives and measures;
- allow for comment against each objective;
- provide for overall supervisor comment;
- incorporate overall employee comment, including opportunity for upward feedback;
- include next level manager overview;
- provide for grievance mechanism;
- support by training and peer discussion strategies to avoid bias;
- include full scale descriptions when rating scales used.

Performance Recognition
- Consider intrinsic and extrinsic reward.
- Provide continuous coaching and feedback.
- Provide acknowledgement, celebration of achievement close to event.
- Consider:
  - Special training opportunities;
  - Job rotation opportunities;
  - Acting in higher grade opportunities;
  - Incremental advancement;
  - Special recognition awards, e.g. employee of the year.

Performance Pay
- Needs careful design to avoid it becoming a disincentive.
- Requires robust appraisal tool.
- Needs monitoring of outcomes.
- Design should support business strategies.
- Use skill based pay only is agency requires development and use of new skills.
- Use competency pay with base pay model if the competencies provide value added to the agency.
- Link increments of merit pay schemes to performance.
- Provide rewards for **individuals** and **teams** where appropriate.

IMPLEMENTING THE SYSTEM

DEFINING OWNERSHIP AND RESOURCES

Implementing a new or changed performance management approach is a major organisational intervention that requires careful planning and resourcing. Ownership and resourcing issues will need to be resolved at the initial stage of a performance management project.

During the development and design stage of the project, it is best if the 'owners' of the system are close to and have the influence and resourcing power of a strong sponsor. At this stage, the project is often 'owned' within the Prime Minister's Department or is managed by the key public reform project team.

Once the system has been implemented, it is generally 'owned', monitored and maintained by the area that manages other human resource management policies.

Resourcing during research and development needs to include adequate high-level sponsorship and technical expertise and allocation of tasks to encourage ownership across the public sector and input into the system. A project-resourcing model, found to be successful in a number of settings, is the utilisation of a Heads of Department Steering Committee supported by a Dedicated Project Team and Across Department Consultative Group.

Once the system is implemented, it needs to be recognised that, in order to be effective, it will require on-going maintenance and monitoring of the relevant tasks included in the job descriptions and work plans of appropriate personnel.

DEVELOPING AN IMPLEMENTATION PLAN

A project plan is ideally developed at the earliest possible stage of performance management introduction or upgrade. The plan will be required to guide pre-, during and post-implementation stages of the project. The plan needs to include detailed activities, timelines and responsibilities for each stage of the project. Development of the Performance Management Project Plan will serve to clarify ownership and resourcing issues and allow a reality check on what is required to be done, what resources need to be committed, and what timeframes are appropriate. An example of part of a Performance Management Project Plan is given below.

Performance Management Project Plan

Focus – Communication Activity – Development of System Objective		
Tasks	**Responsibility**	**Timeframe**
Research organisation's direction statements		
Research of best practice in Performance Management		
Conduct of discussion segment at senior management meeting		
Development of submission to Executive		

Performance Management Project Plan. Example only of possible section.

WHAT TO INCLUDE IN THE PROJECT PLAN

Develop the project plan to include all tasks needed to prepare the way, develop, implement and maintain the new or upgraded performance management approach.

A useful approach to project plan development is to identify a series of major activity focus headings under which the tasks can be logically grouped in time sequence order. A suggested list of headings is Communication, System

Design, System Implementation, System Training and System Institutionalisation.

A checklist of tasks to consider, under each focus heading, for inclusion in a Performance Management Project Plan is provided below:

Plan Checklist

Focus – Communication
- Development of system objective
- Key stakeholder and audience analysis
- Key Message development for each audience
- Delivery mediums and timeframes for each audience
- Development of strategies for Design, Introduction and Maintenance stages of project

Focus – Design
- Research design options (government guidelines, best practice, other systems)
- Consider fit and integration with other planning and HR systems
- Undertake employee testing
- Provide user-friendly documentation
- Co-ordinate communication/consultation strategies in communication plan
- Deal with training, career development, grievance and confidentiality issues

Focus – System Implementation
- Identify pilot sites (if appropriate)
- Prepare pilot sites – Sponsorship, Corporate Plans, Business Plans, reporting relationships, position descriptions
- Develop support communication strategies in the communication plan
- Provide support for supervisors during introduction

Focus – System Training
Identify number of employees to be trained
Identify number of supervisors to be trained
Identify training resources
Design training courses
Train all staff who will provide support during implementation
Train all users

Focus – System Institutionalisation
- Evaluate
- Identify on-going system owner
- Monitor outcomes/Audit
- Investigate unusual outcomes
- Provide additional training support as required
- Upgrade system as required
- Align with budgetary planning cycle

COMMUNICATION IS IMPORTANT

Performance management systems impact on issues central to the work life of every employee. These issues include what work performance is expected, how people will be managed and rewarded and how performance difficulties will be dealt with.

Communication is therefore a critical activity in developing a performance management system. Communication will be needed to inform and encourage support for the change from sponsors, management and employees.

Key communication questions to ask in developing communication tasks include:

- Who are the audiences?
- What are their issues?
- What do we want them to know and understand?
- How can we best deliver the information?

Strategies may include information sessions; information bulletins to staff; inclusion of performance management questions and answers in staff newsletters; and use of performance management information hotlines during system implementation.

PERFORMANCE MANAGEMENT TRAINING

THE KEY ROLE IN TRAINING AND SUCCESSFUL IMPLEMENTATION

The introduction of Performance Management often demands a radical departure from old styles of managing and being managed.

A key element of organisational and public sector reform worldwide has been shifted away from authoritarian management styles to a more consultative approach. There is recognition that, in order to survive in an era of constant change, organisations need to encourage input from every employee.

Performance Management, with its emphasis on jointly agreeing work plans at the start of the performance year, coaching and problem-solving, progress discussions and open appraisal, is dependent for its success on an open, consultative and supportive management approach.

Such an approach often requires major shifts in attitude by both managers and employees. Experience, over time, of the usefulness of the new approach is needed to achieve attitude change. However, pre-implementation training will give managers and employees the information and skills needed to overcome initial fear and resistance and enable them to carry out the performance management processes successfully.

Pre-implementation training for everyone (all managers/supervisors and employees who will participate in the performance management system) is seen as a prerequisite for the implementation of performance management.

It has been found useful to divide Performance Management training requirements into a number of phases:

- Performance Management sensitisation (pre-implementation);
- Training of trainers and implementation staff (pre-implementation);
- Training of managers/supervisors and employees (pre-implementation);
- Integration of Performance Management training into the on-going training curriculum (post-implementation).

PERFORMANCE MANAGEMENT SENSITISATION TRAINING

Sensitisation activities are designed to overcome initial opposition and misunderstandings, prior to implementation of the new performance management system. These activities may overlap and support communication and system consultation and testing activities.

Sensitisation training commonly takes the form of briefing sessions, presentations or workshops. Novel tactics such as the use of videos and street theatre have also been employed.

The session will ideally include an opportunity to ask questions. This will both satisfy audience needs and provide an opportunity for a comprehensive question and answer script to be developed to inform other phases of the training and system implementation.

All key stakeholders, including system sponsors and employee associations as well as future system users need to be included in the sensitisation training.

Sensitisation sessions are often of short duration, commonly from between two hours to half a day.

TRAINING OF TRAINERS AND IMPLEMENTATION STAFF

The prerequisite need for all participants to be trained before commencing their first Performance Management cycle often leads to a scarcity of training resources. A well-accepted solution is to develop a Train the Trainer in Performance Management approach. This involves the identification and training of suitable and training of suitable trainers across departments. Once trained, the trainers work in pairs to present training courses throughout the public sector. Ideally, one trainer in each pair will be from the performance management project team and one from the department in which the training is being carried out.

A typical Train the Trainer in Performance Management course would provide understanding of:

- adult learners and adult learning techniques

- facilitating groups and giving presentations
- developing and guiding Performance Management course participants in:
    - understanding Performance Management principles;
    - understanding the new Performance system;
    - acquiring a knowledge of the benefits of the Performance system;
    - gaining the ability to participate effectively in the processes of the system;
    - assisting their staff (where relevant) to participate effectively in the processes of the system;
    - carrying out performance reviews (where relevant) in a fair and unbiased manner.

Participants selected for the Train the Trainer in Performance Management will ideally already have completed some form of training techniques, presentation or facilitation skills course and be representative of the range of departments across the public sector.

Train the Trainer in Performance Management courses can vary in length, depending on the pre-knowledge of the participants. A minimum of five days is recommended.

Implementation Staff

It is necessary to train Performance Management implementation staff to provide them with the ability to answer questions accurately and to provide support to managers/supervisors and employees during system implementation.

Training of implementation staff would encompass:

- principles of Performance Management;
- processes of the new system;
- skill development in formulating objectives and performance measures;
- understanding bias-free rating;
- their role in handling Performance Management enquiries;
- procedural issues relating to confidentiality, handling and storage of system documents and dealing with grievances;
- common questions and answers relating to the new system.

Performance Management implementation staff will be members of the Project Team, the Across-Department Consultative Group or of departmental human resource areas. They are people who will be required to play and active support role in providing materials and advice during implementation of the system.

A course length of three days would be required to cover required topics for this group.

TRAINING OF MANAGERS/SUPERVISORS AND EMPLOYEES

The conduct of training for all participants is an important and complex logistical step that needs to be undertaken before participants prepare their first performance management work plan.

Options to spread training and administrative resources further include introducing the performance system in gradual stages across the public sector or staggering the start date in the first performance year. This approach allows participants to commence their performance year when they have completed the training course.

Separate courses are generally developed and conducted for managers/ supervisors (those who will conduct appraisals and be appraised) and employees (those who will be appraised only). Managers/supervisors conducting appraisals have a more complex task and require additional course content. In addition, employees have been found to participate more actively in the training sessions when their supervisors are not present.

It has also been found that training people at the same seniority level from similar areas is a successful means of facilitating course participants to share learning during and after the course.

Typical Performance Management courses for managers/supervisors and employees would include:

Managers/supervisors
- understanding principles of Performance Management;
- understanding benefits and processes of the new system;
- drawing departmental work plans from the Business Plan;

- skills development in formulating objectives and performance measures;
- providing on-going coaching for employees;
- recognising, managing and improving unsatisfactory performance;
- conducting objective appraisal interviews;
- completing the appraisal form and using the rating scale fairly and accurately.

Employees
- understanding principles of Performance Management;
- understanding benefits and processes of the new system;
- skills development in formulating objectives and performance measures;
- developing draft performance work plans;
- participating in Performance Management interviews.

Course participants will be all members of the public secotr who will participate in the performance management processes.

Course length will vary depending on culture and expected learning rates. A minimum of one and a half days would be required for manager/supervisor training and one day for employee training.

INTEGRATION OF PERFORMANCE MANAGEMENT TRAINING INTO THE ON-GOING TRAINING CURRICULUM

Once the initial pre-implementation training phases are completed, it is important to the on-going success of the system that Performance Management training is institutionalised as part of the on-going training and skills development approach of the public sector.

This can be achieved by:

- including Performance Management training as part of the induction of new entrants to the service;

- including Performance Management and Performance Management-related segments as on-going development modules in supervisor and management courses. Segments in support of a performance approach might include leadership, strategic planning, project planning, communication, meeting and interview skills, negotiation skills, managing for continuous improvement and a focus on customer service quality.

INSTITUTIONALISATION OF THE PERFORMANCE MANAGEMENT SYSTEM

MAINTENANCE AND MONITORING

A successful performance management system will be an integral part of the fabric of the organisation. It will translate organisational objectives into tasks, outputs and outcomes. It will increase understanding and co-operation between employees and management. Management decision-making and resource allocation will be informed by training needs identified and performance appraisal outcomes generated by the system. Employees will enjoy greater clarity of role and task expectation, supervisor support and fairer performance reward.

Performance management systems are now working in this manner in many successful organisations. However, success can only be achieved through resourcing and maintaining the performance system, not only in the design and implementation phases, but also on an on-going basis.

Retain high-level sponsorship for your system by utilising its full potential as a strategic management planning and information feedback tool.

Ensure that the system policy is maintained in the appropriate policy area and with the required degree of compliance.

Provide on-going support and advice to managers so that they can obtain the full benefits of the system. Consider whether extra training or workshop sessions are needed in areas where difficulties are occurring.

EVALUATION

Evaluation of the system after the pilot or the first two years of operation and then after every five years will help ensure that it continues to be the best possible system for the organisation.

Evaluation methods can include the use of questionnaires, interviews, focus groups and desk research examination of performance documents and outcomes. The Diagnostic Survey detailed in the Needs Analysis section of this publication can also be used to evaluate the system.

Actions taken in system development can help to ensure that effective system evaluations can be carried out in the future. These actions include:

- Ensuring programme objectives are developed so that there is a benchmark against which to evaluate.

- Developing a realistic set of desired outcomes or results over particular timeframes for the system from its objectives.

- Develop performance indicators to measure outcomes.

System evaluation can be enhanced by the consideration of on-going developments in Performance Management best practice, including Quality Award criteria for performance management systems. Keeping a check on these and appropriate new developments in other organisations may enhance the system. However, if the system is working well, avoid costly and unnecessary change.

Best Practice Performance Management*

System components, including:

- Individual and team performance.
- Recognition and reward.
- System integration.
- Employee feedback.
- Development opportunities.
- Links to organisational goals.

* Baldridge Award Criteria

MONITORING OUTCOMES

On-going monitoring of the system outcomes will assist in ensuring that the system is being used consistently across departments and in an unbiased manner.

Measures to be considered in monitoring across departments for system use compliance, consistency in use of rating scales, and differential outcomes for any groups at risk of discrimination are detailed below:

- percentage of reviews completed;
- percentage of individuals unsatisfactory;
- percentage of individuals receiving performance pay;
- percentage of affirmative action target groups receiving performance pay.

Annual statistical monitoring of Performance System outcomes can be carried out by the appropriate central agency or as part of the standard audit process of the Auditor General.

REFERENCES

Performance Management, Michael Armstrong, Kogan Page, London 1997

Pay for Performance, Performance Appraisal and Pay in the APS, The Auditor General, Audit Report No. 16, Canberra, 1993–94

The Handbook of Performance Management, Francis Neale, editor, Institute of Personnel Management, London 1993

People, Performance and Pay, The Hay Group, New York, 1996

Performance Appraisal: Perspectives on a Quality Management Approach, American Society for Training and Development Research Committee, McLean, Damme, Swanson, editors

Performance Appraisals, Martin Fisher, The Sunday Times, Kogan Page, London 1995

Working Towards Results – Managing Individual Performance in the Public Service, Jorm, N., Hunt, J., Manning, N., Commonwealth Secretariat, London 1996 (available through CAPAM).

DESIGNING PERFORMANCE APPRAISAL SYSTEMS

Needs Analysis and Performance Management Systems

Case Study I

Barbados

STEPS FOR PERFORMANCE ANALYSIS

The Barbados Public Service is approximately 23,000 strong, comprising general service personnel, teachers, nurses, police, prison and fire officers as well as personnel of statutory corporations. It is a centrally controlled system with a Public Service Commission and provides for transfers across the service. In addition, there is also a Police Service Commission as well as a Judicial and Legal Services Commission.

The Constitution of Barbados provides for a Public Service Commission and confers on it the responsibility *"for the appointment, promotion, dismissal and disciplinary control of public officers generally,"* with the proviso that *"Permanent Secretaries, heads and deputy heads of government departments can only be appointed with the consent of the Prime Minister"*.

There has been an appraisal system in existence in Barbados for many years and has been modified from time to time to capture information on public service personnel below the level of top management.

Within this system, temporary officers are assessed on elements listed in the form below.

STAFF REPORT – TEMPORARY OFFICERS

Part 1. Personal Data:

Name of Officer	Post
Ministry/department	
Period of Report: From:	To:

Part 11. Performance Rating:

Key to Rating: A – Outstanding B –Very Good C – Good D – Satisfactory E – Not Quite Satisfactory F – Unsatisfactory

Elements of performance	Rating				Remarks
1. Personal appearance					
2. Relations with colleagues					
3. Relations with the public					
4. Output of work					
5. Quality of work					
6. Organisation of own work					
7. Assumption of responsibility					
8. Initiative					
Overall Performance					

On the other hand, the performance of Appointed Officers is assessed on elements listed in the form below:

Part 2. REPORT ON PERFORMANCE DURING RATING PERIOD

2.a   Performance rating (to be completed by reporting officer)

- Reporting officer should consult any other officer regarding supervising the reportee for a period longer than three months during the reporting period.

- Present posts (not acting posts) on both the reporting & countersigning officers must be above that of the officer on whom the report is made.

Key to Rating: A – Outstanding B – Very Good C – Good D – Satisfactory E – Not Quite Satisfactory F – Satisfactory

Elements of performance	Rating A – F					Remarks
Knowledge of job - - - -						
Quality of Work - - - - -						
Productivity - - - - - - - -						
Co-operation - - - - - - - -						
Initiative - - - - - - - - - - -						
Management of Subordinates						
Overall grading - - - - - - -						

2.b   Other assessment

Fitness for promotion:

(a) This officer is capable of performing the duties at a higher grade –

    Satisfactorily   Very well   exceptionally well

    OR

(b) This officer is not capable at the present time of performing the duties of a higher grade

    He/She is –

    Likely to be capable in time   Likely to have reached his/her limits

---

This system is highly subjective. It makes provision for an assessment of personal characteristics, and bears no linkage to organisational objectives. Assessments, in this context, are not consistent and have no impact on individual or organisational productivity. In the circumstances, it is also unclear what effect these assessments have had on promotions, transfers and training.

The forms for these assessments are completed annually and make provision for the employee to accept the assessment or set out any disagreements. There is, however, no provision for corrective feedback.

RATIONALE FOR INTRODUCING APPRAISAL SYSTEMS

It is necessary for every organisation to have some means of appraising its employees which should be fair and unbiased, give management some understanding of how each employee is performing, and help to motivate the employee. Such knowledge can assist in promotions, transfers, training, and separation. In addition, this information provides for the better management of human resources, allows for relevant training to take place, and appropriate deployment compatible with skills that ultimately lead to greater productivity.

In 1995, the Government of Barbados reiterated the principle that to achieve its development objectives, it would require a fully responsive public service; one infused with new values, a sense of mission and purpose, and totally imbued with the spirit of "professionalism" – the White Paper on Public Sector Reform.

To achieve this, it was necessary to develop a Performance Management System that would bring about the following:

i)   Change to an achievement-driven performance culture through an emphasis on results and employee/manager communication, understanding and commitment;

ii) Better planning through the processes of identifying and linking the objectives and strategies of the organisation to the tasks of each public servant;

iii) Better understanding of work through the clarification of individual work tasks and responsibility boundaries as each public servant's key work tasks for a year, and what will be expected of him/her is identified;

iv) Increased trust through participation in work planning and on-going discussion, feed-back and open appraisal;

v)   Less duplication of effort and wastage of resources through improved work planning;

vi) Turnaround of unsatisfactory performance through on-going feedback and discussion throughout the performance management cycle;

vii) A comprehensive data source to allow organisational skills development and training needs to be clearly identified and prioritised;

viii) A cost-effective data source for targeted employee development, recognition and reward programmes;

ix) A planning and measurement system that allows for organisational, divisional, team and individual performance indicators and measures as well as generic indicators which can be used to encourage co-operative and other desired organisational behaviours;

x)   A system that can be linked with other management reform programmes such as ethics, competency development and quality programmes to provide a comprehensive human resource management framework;

xi)   A performance culture that is also an equity culture with decisions relating to employees based on information about results and not whether they are liked or disliked.

THE REQUIRED PERFORMANCE STANDARDS

It was recognised that there was need to have an appraisal system that was objective, unbiased and took the needs of both the employee and the organisation into account. A vital component of this would be agreed performance standards that would flow out of an up-to-date job description which is structured to allow the employee to meet the specific objectives of the ministry/department. In most instances, there was a need to measure both quality and quantity. In many areas of public administration, these standards are somewhat difficult to clarify since they seldom deal with matters as easy to measure as increased sales in a private sector company or improved production, yet there must be agreement on organisational objectives and performance standards so that it can be easily concluded whether the employee has reached agreed targets. It therefore means that a great deal of work has to be put in at the beginning, in training and setting up the system, to allow for the smooth running of the system.

The problem here is that the process requires a deep understanding of the organisational objectives and what each employee must contribute. In some instances, the Productivity Council had attempted to set up Key Performance Indicators (KPI) for some organisations in an effort to measure productivity, but those KPIs had never been translated into individual goals or individual performance standards.

The first problem was arriving at up-to-date job descriptions, breaking them down element-by-element and setting objective standards for measurement. It is an important task that needed to be done by every supervisor, but it makes everything so much easier after the job has been done. It was easier of course to set standards for the secretary/typist because a great deal of her work could be quantified, but not so easy for administrative officers who carry out research, draft documents and take minutes of meetings. The exercise is always easier when it can be quantified.

Any credible performance appraisal system must be tied to stated objectives, agreed upon by the employee and the head of the ministry/department within the context of the overall objectives of the ministry and department. Employees must be appraised on the basis of task accomplishment. It is mandatory for the appraiser to communicate with the employee and conduct structured interviews on a regular and on-going basis.

Satisfactory performance should be rewarded, while unsatisfactory performance should result in corrective measures developed through a performance improvement plan.

POTENTIAL CAUSES OF THE PROBLEM

Moving to a new culture of Performance Management requires a great deal of designing, training and marketing. Current systems are normally fully embedded, and although they may be highly criticised by management and employees alike, they are normally safe and threaten no one. However, a new system, which would deal with issues of planning, performance, productivity, recognition, reward and separation could be quite overwhelming.

It was recognised that difficulties would arise in trying to persuade employees that there was an advantage in moving away from a safe automatic incremental system to one based on performance. From discussions that had already begun as to whether the appraisal system being developed for teachers should be formative or summative, it was obvious that there would be problems in convincing public servants generally that this system was not being designed to get rid of them and reduce the size of the public service. There was strong contention, especially from the Unions, that appraisals could only be used for the development of the employee, and not for the dismissal of the employee.

Some departments had already begun to develop their own systems and would need to be convinced that any new system was better than the one they were developing or that it could incorporate the work they had already done. In addition, some technical and professional divisions saw themselves as unique and would therefore require special consideration.

EXAMPLES

Designing the form has its own problems, for although the needs analysis clearly indicates what needs to be done, some stakeholders are sometimes reluctant to go along with proposals that would affect them, especially if they believe that they will be affected negatively. The effort requires the allocation of resources to provide training. A core group of trainers had to be prepared to carry out the training service-wide. Even scheduling presented some large logistical problems.

Marketing is important to the success of the programme. It is an on-going process requiring on-going communication and a response to all legitimate concerns. The organisation leading the process must be in a position to show how the system can improve the work of the organisation and be of advantage to the employee. All users of the system must be confident that the appraisal will always be consistent and fair.

There were also problems associated with the old system which the new system would have to seek to correct. Surely, it would need to address the fact that the form was not:

(i)   completed more than once per year;
(ii)   completed in consultation with the employee;
(iii)   an instrument of development at the ministry/department level, but was forwarded to a central personnel agency when completed – for filing;
(iv)   used to provide feed-back or follow-up;
(v)   properly completed, so that very little could be found in them to deal with disciplinary cases when they occurred.

The result of all of this is that the form was falling into disuse since it appeared to have no direct bearing on people's careers. It did not even provide a rationale for transfers within the service, which is one of the issues that pained many civil servants. The new system would surely address what many junior staff referred to as 'unexplained supercession', which demoralised staff. The system should therefore bring some transparency to the situation in which seniority appeared to be the main consideration. The new system would identify those employees who were performing well and should be promoted.

TASK IDENTIFICATION

TASKS NOT BEING PERFORMED

It was necessary to carry out a comprehensive needs analysis to get a clear picture of the actual situation throughout the service, to determine what needed to be done and how it should be done. It was also necessary to build consensus for a new system.

It was discovered that some departments were already experimenting with new Forms of Appraisal, while others were practising or ignoring the current system. For one, many of the technical departments felt that the present system did not assist them in measuring the necessary competencies or routines important to the tasks, critical to their work; and none of the systems was really measuring performance.

Although there was a requirement for the forms to be completed annually, in many instances, it was not complied with. When the requirement was met, the forms were sometimes held up in the ministry/department and not forwarded to the central personnel division. Those that were duly returned, were kept on file, to be used if needed. There was no real importance attaching to this exercise, except for the fact that employees saw remarks on their reports with which they disagreed or with which they had been unaware until then. The maid, at the end of the year, discovered that she had not cleaned the sinks properly one day; the administrative officer learnt that he was a clock-watcher; and the secretary that her typing had too many errors.

There was little emphasis on setting standards for organisations or for employees, so there was no standard for the time a passport would take to process, the time it would take to get a birth certificate, the processing of applications made to the Town and Country Planning Department. There were no sanctions in place to encourage compliance. No consistent effort was being made to improve performance in spite of the fact that the public was demanding better and quicker service and there was general agreement that Barbados needed to become more competitive.

POSITIONS RESPONSIBLE FOR PERFORMING TASKS

The task of conducting performance appraisals of employees rests mainly with the central personnel agency working through permanent secretaries, heads of departments and supervisors. The central personnel agency, acting on behalf of the Public Service Commissions, needed to convince permanent secretaries, heads of departments and employees of the importance of the system, that it was being used effectively and was the basis for all promotions, transfers, training and discipline.

The task of changing from a system where forms are completed by the supervisor with the head of the department/permanent secretary endorsing the completed form, to a system which requires greater planning, greater open communication and agreement on approach and expectations is quite difficult. It requires the development of new job descriptions, which are comprehensive, as well as task and performance-related.

In the new system, the immediate supervisor and the head of department continues to play the role they have been traditionally playing – that of supervising and reporting. In addition, the minister and/or the head of civil service would now be responsible for assessing top managers who were not formerly assessed.

To begin the process of developing a new system of appraisal, a steering committee on Performance Management was set up to examine the need for a new system, as well as to design and implement a new system of appraisals. The Committee comprised a wide cross-section of stakeholders and was chaired by the permanent secretary in the Ministry of the Civil Service, who had responsibility for co-ordinating the national Public Sector Reform Programme. The committee included the head of the civil service, the chief personnel officer, who is also the chief adviser to the Public Service Commission, permanent secretaries and heads of departments from key ministries and departments to cover as many areas of government as possible without becoming too large or unmanageable. A representative of the unions was included as well as officers working on improved systems of appraisals for their ministries/departments.

It was recognised at once that there would be need for a consultant, preferably one with international experience, who could assist in the needs analysis and in the design of a system to meet the needs of the public service, develop training materials and ensure that a thorough programme for trainers was carried out. A great deal of discussion arose over what type of system would be appropriate for Barbados, and the following options were examined:

a) A generic system – one appraisal system to be used by everyone in the public service: the completed forms to be sent to the central agency annually; the forms to be used for assessing training and development needs and for promotional purposes; or

b) A generic system – a system of appraisal with a number of different appraisal forms and guidelines developed for job categories: clerical, general management, teachers, police, probation officers, social workers, health professionals, financial professionals etc.: common formats to be used across the Service, to be completed and sent to the central agency – the Ministry of the Civil Service – annually to be used for assessing training and development needs and for promotional purposes.

c) Guidelines – detailed guidelines drawn up for ministries to follow in developing their own appraisal systems. This would allow each ministry to use different appraisal forms, and conduct their appraisal management somewhat differently, but assure consistency since each ministry's performance appraisal system would be required to adhere to the guidelines. To ensure consistency and fairness, each ministry would be required to submit its forms and process to the Ministry of the Civil Service for review. The completed forms would be retained by the ministry and assist them in developing training and development needs, with a copy being sent to the Ministry of the Civil Service to assist in the promotion of employees.

WHAT IS REQUIRED PERFORMANCE?

It was generally agreed that the present system needed upgrading, but some divisions considered themselves so unique that they either required a tailor-made system or recognition of their uniqueness within any new system.

One ministry, a technical division, the Police Service, had already designed systems and forms, and discussions needed to take place to determine whether the new system would include their needs.

In the new system, each employee/manager would be expected to meet 80 per cent or more of agreed objectives and demonstrate overall required behaviours, and any functional competencies at a satisfactory level or above. Of course, performance could exceed expectations as well, as it could be "outstanding". Consistency in rating must also be achieved if the system is going to be effective.

The rating of performances goes from 'meets expectations' to 'exceeds expectations', to 'outstanding' on the positive side and on the negative, to 'needs development' to 'unacceptable'. There was a strong argument for a range of three moving from 'meeting expectations' to 'exceeding expectations' or on the other hand, 'not meeting expectations'. However in the end, it was agreed that there must be provision to accommodate the 'outstanding' as well as those who 'need development' from those whose performance was 'unacceptable'.

In each case, the required performance would include meeting performance measures, based on job descriptions as well as demonstrated behaviours which would be classified under general work conduct; knowledge of job; managing work; team work; and customer service. For employees holding positions that require degrees or diplomas: professionalism; management behaviour; ongoing learning; and leadership must also be assessed.

In short, required performance is what each department, through its supervisors, expects of each employee in the fulfillment of the organisation's goals. A clerical officer might be expected to file accurately and retrieve promptly. In many cases, performance was measured in traditional terms of promptness, accuracy, clearance time, and avoidance of errors.

The secretary will be measured against the quality of her typing, the correctness of her work, the way she manages meetings, supports her manager and handles all customers. It should be pointed out that this required performance also required higher performance from those who demanded it. For example, secretaries would only agree to these standards in typing if all manuscripts reaching them were clear, legible and complete.

Administrative officers must be able to complete assignments accurately within the target time.

Supervisors, of course, must not only demonstrate a sound knowledge of the work being done, but must also hold the respect of colleagues and those supervised. In addition, the supervisor must be able to deal with staff fairly and be able to motivate them. Promptness, accuracy and thoroughness will also be elements of the required standards. As it turned out, required performance called for better customer service and greater accountability.

WHEN DID THE PROBLEM FIRST OCCUR AND WHERE?

The identification of the tasks was easy, but the problem arose where some stakeholders felt that the present system had merit and should therefore be upgraded. Other stakeholders felt that one system could not meet the needs of the whole service and that a system was required that would allow for comparisons of personnel performance across the service. In addition, when the extent of the work was spelt out, its magnitude and the implications of the new system for managers and employees modified the enthusiasm.

There were still other technical areas, such as assessing the performance of Air Traffic Controllers, which would require more specificity in the evaluation to determine whether technical requirements were being met on a daily and on-going basis. They were, however, willing to buy into the system.

In the case of the Department of Civil Aviation, the required performance was to ensure that technical officers, for example Air Traffic Controllers, carried out their tasks efficiently and competently. These include separation of aircraft, promptness of action to correct errors, adherence to standard procedures, correctness of computer entries etc. Nurses and police also needed to evaluate promptness, accuracy, clearance time and avoidance of errors.

WHAT ARE THE SYMPTOMS OF THE PROBLEM

It was obvious that there was deep insecurity and doubt as to whether a system could be designed that could meet all the needs of the Barbados Public Service, be fair, unbiased and consistent. What guarantees were there that it could it be credible and remain credible? How would it be possible for supervisors to arrive at agreement with employees on what was the employee's role in meeting the objectives of the organisation and how performance would be measured.

The source of the problem really resided in the fact that there was no consistent or co-ordinated effort made to achieve individual objectives prior to this effort. The present practice made people sceptical about whether such a level of credibility could be achieved. Would there be any action taken against heads of departments who were mismanaging? How could favouritism be detected and removed in a small country where everyone knows everyone else and may even be related in some way, and where confidential information may quite easily be circulated? Would supervisors have the confidence of their convictions or would they be afraid to record the truth and deal with the issues? Would there be opportunities for political interference and how could these be dealt with? Seniority could not be argued with, but other merit systems always bring with them the fear that one could be overlooked.

SOLUTION

PROCESS OF CONSULTATION AND CO-ORDINATION

It was obvious that it was necessary to consult far and wide to determine not only the kind and type of system required to meet the needs of a varied, complex service but also to win support for the new system.

A process was started across ministry, vertically and horizontally, to outline the issues as well as achieve feedback for the development of such a system. Every effort was made to appreciate the work that had already been done, and to make use of any features that worked satisfactorily.

It was thought too, that if the new system could be linked to the Programme Performance Budgeting System, which was being introduced at the time, that each could complement and enhance the other. A collaborative effort was therefore started between the Ministry of Finance and the Ministry of the Civil Service to achieve this end, and to link the budget to organisational objectives.

The process of consultation began with the consultant holding discussions with various ministries, departments and unions, seeking to understand their needs, dealing with their concerns and seeking to incorporate their requirements into a system wherever possible.

The broad-based committee on performance appraisal, including representatives from across the service as well as union representatives, discussed the various proposals, made changes and approved the system and the form. Discussions were then held at ministry and department levels to introduce the form to the decision-makers.

In the meantime, the form was submitted formally to Cabinet to seek approval in principle for the implementation of such a system. It was agreed that details, which still needed to be negotiated, would be submitted later for approval. These included sanctions and a system for reward and recognition.

At the same time, the union was asked to study the proposed system so that it would enjoy their support.

STRATEGIES TO IMPROVE PERFORMANCE

It was recognised that any credible Performance Appraisal System would require organisations to develop new strategic plans. Organisational reviews would follow to determine organisational goals from which the individual role of all employees would flow; and relevant job descriptions would be developed to ensure that performance was relevant to organisational goals and could be measured.

The strategies to improve performance were to give employees realistic objectives, recognise inadequacies early, provide corrective assistance, motivate with a view to ensuring that the round pegs found round holes and square pegs, square ones. Recognition for good performance would also have to be an integral part of the system.

Efforts were made to move all ministries to develop or review their strategic plans before the date of implementation. Within this framework, it was expected that not only mission statements would be updated, but the role of each employee would be defined. Some ministries and departments were reluctant to commence the exercise. Some felt they already had their plans, and need not undertake the exercise; and others complained of not having the resources to do so. A decision was taken that the central ministries – the ministries dealing with finance and personnel – should take the lead, and especially the Ministry of the Civil Service which was co-ordinating the Public Sector Reform programme. It was obviously necessary to lead by example.

This too had its setbacks, since two of the leading permanent secretaries were leaving the Service soon after this exercise. A change of any personnel and direction could set back the process. However, it gave the ministry implementing the new system an opportunity to work out operating problems and have first hand knowledge of what they might be. The undertaking also helped in selling the system, since other ministries and departments were persuaded by the fact that the ministry co-ordinating the implementation of the system was also a user of the system.

It was felt that the Performance Appraisal System would impact directly on the Public Sector Reform programme that was under way. The objectives of that programme, which are consistent with the objectives of the appraisal systems, were summarised in the White Paper on Public Sector Reform as follows:

i)   Promote productivity throughout the public sector.
ii)   Refocus government towards the necessary redefinition of the respective roles of the public and private sectors in the emerging social and economic order.
iii)   Optimise the use of resources.
iv)   Achieve improved levels of accountability.
v)   Create standards of performance that will promote job satisfaction and increased level of competitiveness.
vi)   Transform the public sector into an efficient and effective organisation.
vii)   Improve systems and procedures to make them more relevant to modern public sector management.
viii)   Value for money: improving the quality of goods and services delivered by the public sector to its customers.
ix)   Establish requisite training programmes to enhance management and performance skills at all levels of the public sector.

The Performance Appraisal System was designed to bring about the objectives listed above, since it would force organisations to have clear objectives, and supervisors and supervisees to be clear about the tasks and performance measures required to meet these objectives. It would assist in identifying required skills for each job, provide help to those who needed it, and re-deploy those who needed re-deploying. It would also formally identify those who needed to be placed in employee assistance programmes at an early date, and demand more productive behaviour.

The need to carry out strategic planning and review mission statements is a logical first step in re-focusing government. Up-dating job descriptions and identifying the role of each employee, supervisor or manager would not only restructure organisations, but would support the focus, cut out wastage and identify skills necessary for the organisation to operate successfully. Emphasising performance and training to correct shortcomings would improve productivity. Recognition and reward would help to motivate employees at all levels and encourage higher performance. Fairness and transparency in the system would also give employees job satisfaction. Ultimately, placing the round pegs in the round holes would bring about a high performance organisation. It would also provide for better human resource management in a decentralised and organised manner.

In addition, the improvement of performance of the individual and the organisation in a focused manner should bring about greater productivity and competitiveness in the public service and also higher levels of customer satisfaction for the public at large.

INVOLVEMENT OF STAKEHOLDERS (e.g. staff associations)

Stakeholders were identified as public servants, supervisors and managers, unions representing public servants, the political directorate, the Public Service Commission, the Chief Personnel Officer, and the Ministry of the Civil Service. Effort was therefore made to involve them at every stage of development and implementation. A special meeting of permanent secretaries was convened and seminars were held for deputy permanent secretaries, heads of departments and personnel responsible for personnel matters, as well as officers of various levels who were selected from across the service.

The Steering Committee not only included personnel from key ministries and departments, but also a representative selected by the trade unions. In addition, proposals were formally submitted to the unions for consideration, while presentations were made to the Public Service Commission, the Social Partners and the Cabinet for approval.

Some departments were enthusiastic about being in the forefront of this exercise. They immediately recognised the need for such a system. Those who were working towards an instrument of their own thought that the proposal could not have come at a better time.

Other departments preferred a pilot approach. They wanted to wait and see. The problem with such a wait-and-see approach is the length of time it takes to pilot and draw lessons, and then implement elsewhere. Very often, it does not benefit those who are waiting to see the results of the pilot.

In the meantime, staff from the central personnel agencies were sent on a mission to observe a performance appraisal system in action. This was to prepare the central agencies to organise the proper management of the system.

Co-ordination of the process was not an easy task. Very few organisations agreed with the timetable. They wanted more time to deal with the programme. An effort was made to establish a date and link it to the budgetary process to give it some relevance and some teeth, but this slipped and the implementation process had to be extended. In the circumstances, it lost some of the excitement, but it gave the organisations more time to plan and prepare for the system.

DESIGNING NEW PERFORMANCE APPRAISAL SYSTEMS

The Performance Review and Development system was designed with very clear objectives. These were to:

i)   link the tasks of each department and each employee to the key tasks and key results for each agency;

ii)   provide
        (a) a set of required behaviours aimed at the development of employee skills and behaviours required to achieve "new professionalism,"

        (b) processes for improved work planning, which would clarify authority, responsibility, reporting and accountability relationships;

        (c) opportunities for improved dialogue between managers, supervisors and employees;

iii)   identify competence and allow for the prioritisation of training and development needs of employees;

iv)   encourage early identification and turnaround of unsatisfactory performance;

v)   recognise and reward good performance through appreciation and incentive awards and opportunities for career development; and

vi)   appraise the performance of all employees in a transparent, objective, fair and consistent manner.

The form was therefore designed to achieve these objectives set out above which should in turn bring about greater organisational effectiveness, greater customer satisfaction and greater competitiveness in the public sector.

In addition to measuring performance by meeting the objectives of the organisation, all employees are assessed on:

(a)   general work conduct;
(b)   knowledge of the job;
(c)   management of work;
(d)   team-work;
(e)   customer service.

There is also provision for employees holding positions which require a professional qualification such as a degree or diploma to be assessed, as well as the management performance, on-going learning, and leadership of supervisors and managers.

PROCESS OF APPRAISING MANAGERS (e.g. permanent secretaries)

It should be noted that the system was designed to cover the whole public service. National objectives, handed down through ministries and departments, would be translated into specific Objectives and Key Performance Indicators, which would guide the formulation of ministry/department business plans and individual/ employee work-plans.

Every member of the public service would therefore be expected to develop a work-plan with the immediate supervisor or manager, receive coaching and assistance throughout the year, and be reviewed on the achievement of agreed work plan objectives and the demonstration of required behaviours at the end of the review year.

All managers, including permanent secretaries, are to be appraised under this system with heads of departments being appraised by the permanent secretary to the ministry. There was some debate as to who should appraise permanent secretaries; whether they would be appraised by their peers, by their immediate minister, by the Head of the Civil Service or by the ministers and Head of Civil Service. It is expected that this should be resolved by the Head of the Civil Service, in consultation with ministers and Prime Minister.

Whatever the result, officers at the next level, like all other employees will have an opportunity to express their satisfaction or dissatisfaction with the management of the permanent secretary and head of department. It is hoped that this will provide valuable feedback for top managers and supervisors who should seek to correct the behaviour that has been identified by the returns.

APPRAISAL SYSTEMS FOR MIDDLE AND LOWER LEVEL MANAGERS

The system is designed so that it can accommodate the appraisal of middle and lower level managers who, like all other public officers, will be appraised by their immediate supervisor/manager.

There was some discussion as to whether middle and lower level managers should be appraised along the same lines as top managers and there was consensus that their overall assessment should be based on the same elements. It was agreed ultimately that middle and lower level managers would be assessed on overall management, which would include handling the staff, financial and budgetary management and communication skills. In addition to this, senior level managers would be assessed on leadership, which would evaluate judgement and vision. All persons, however, would be rated on meeting objectives, required behaviours and functional competencies.

ROLE OF THE SUPERVISOR AND SUPERVISEE

The roles of the supervisor and supervisee are formalised and spelt out in guidelines, which ensure that the supervisor undertakes certain activities before conducting the Performance Review meeting. Before the meeting, all supervisors are expected to refresh their knowledge of the Performance and Development System, the rating process, and the implications for rating. They should also consult with other human resource professionals in their ministries/departments to remove any doubts in their minds.

It is incumbent upon the supervisor to set the time and the place, and to give advance notice to the supervisee of any arrangements for any related meeting. Supervisors must also consider how well they believe those they supervise have performed and make notes for discussion within the meeting. In addition, the supervisor must ensure that the supervisees fully understand the performance review processes and the relationship of the performance rating scale to the achievement of objectives, as described on the performance review form.

In the same manner, the supervisee is expected to prepare for the meeting by considering how well objectives have been met, and the required behaviours have been demonstrated. Consideration must be given to how well the objectives have been achieved and what rating is appropriate. Details of any achievements should also be noted down and be brought to the review meeting. In the meeting, each objective and how well it has been achieved should be discussed in turn and the comments inserted in the work plan form. A total rating can then be agreed upon for the achievement of objectives in line with the objectives rating scale at the bottom of the work plan form.

Demonstration of required behaviours should then be considered, with a rating being given by the supervisor against each behaviour. An overall rating for each required behaviour should be given, based on the most common rating for each behaviour and placed in the rating box below each required behaviour.

If the department has additional functional competencies, which must be assessed, then they should be discussed and a rating given from the functional competencies scale which has been aligned with the performance review scales.

An overall performance rating for the year is then arrived at, based on an equal consideration of performance against agreed objectives, demonstration of required behaviours and group functional competencies. The supervisor then completes the supervisor's comments and ratings section of the form and the supervisee completes the employee's comments section.

The system holds the current supervisor accountable for producing the performance report, although consultation is expected with previous supervisors and other supervisors dealing with the employee's work during the period under review. In addition, supervisors who are leaving a ministry/department/agency because of promotion, transfer, long leave, retirement or termination are required to complete reports for employees who have served with them.

In cases where overall ratings are marginal or unsatisfactory, another meeting must be arranged and held for the purpose of preparing a performance improvement plan to be followed by the employee. In cases where the supervisor and supervisee are unable to reach agreement on the overall rating, the next level manager is invited to assist in the review process.

Where there is disagreement between the supervisor and supervisee, the matter is referred to the next level of management where they seek to resolve the issue to the satisfaction of both the supervisee and supervisor. If this is unsuccessful, the matter must then be referred for resolution by the normal grievance mechanism or procedure practised by the ministry/department. Every effort, however, is made to resolve the matter without resorting to these mechanisms or procedures.

ARE THE CHANGES DIFFERENT FROM THE PREVIOUS SYSTEM?

This system differs from the previous system in approach. The objectives have been discussed and agreed to. The performance criteria have been spelt out, and the outcome allows a developmental plan to be put in place for recognition and/or for promotion.

The previous system was imprecise and although it made an effort to assess knowledge of work, quality of work, and productivity, the range of A–F was far too wide. The basis for the assessment of each element was far too subjective. There was no assessment to determine whether organisational objectives were being met and what were the possible measurements to do so. There have been instances of officers receiving straight As because the assessor wanted to ensure that the officer would be favoured.

The new system requires more planning, and reviews must be done quarterly to determine whether the assessment is on track or whether assistance was required for the employee to meet standards set. Consideration must also be given to whether these standards are realistic and whether the right person is in the job. It provides an opportunity for developmental work to take place, so that at the end of the year, the organisation might have improved its performance because it has been able to identify its personnel problems, and through coaching, counselling and training been able to improve the contribution of the employee and the focus of the job.

The new system is set up to improve the performance of the individual and the organisation to motivate employees for the greater national success.

LINKS WITH REWARD, PROMOTION, ADVANCEMENT AND DISCIPLINE

This system links directly into a system of reward, promotion, transfer and discipline. Employees are rated in a scale of **1** to **5**, where **1** is unacceptable; **2** needs development; **3** meets expectations; **4** exceeds expectations; **5** Outstanding. In this context, **1** and **2** are obviously not satisfactory. Accordingly, employees in this category are not promotable, nor should they receive an increment; **2** however, can benefit from a development plan. **3**, **4**, **5** are not only promotable, but should receive an annual increment with a **4** and a **5** receiving special recognition awards.

There should be recognition for good performance as well as promotion and pay. In a system where there are fixed salary scales as well as increment-based ones, some new approach is necessary to allow all employees – management and otherwise – to be paid for good performance. In such circumstances, automatic increments would have to be discontinued and make way for increments based on performance.

The system also provides the first formal structure for identifying persons whose performance may be affected by tendencies to malinger or by the use of alcohol or drugs. Prior to this, behaviour of this sort was not being dealt with and so it robbed the service of many productive hours. In addition, it has had a demoralising effect on the service. Such behaviour is now provided for within the employee assistance programme.

IMPLEMENTING PERFORMANCE APPRAISAL SYSTEMS

The objectives of the Performance Review and Development System is achieved through a number of initiatives:

- Strategic planning to set direction and to define the long- and short-term objectives at the ministry/department level. Each ministry/department must review its strategic plan and the Ministry of the Office of Public Sector Reform developed a framework and manual to assist ministries in carrying out this exercise. The Ministry of the Civil Service then worked with a number of facilitators to get the process going. It calls for at least four weeks of intensive work and more, especially from those organizations that have not gone through the process before.

- The translation of organisational objectives into work plans for each employee consisting of individual objectives as well as appropriate performance measures and required skill needs. The task proved quite difficult since the old job descriptions were of little assistance. It required new thinking; and even after that, the setting of appropriate measurable performance standards took some persistence. It was clear that the training of managers and supervisors was a priority; they needed to be properly prepared for this critical task. The more intense the training and preparation, the easier the implementation process became.

- The appraisal form identifies a set of required behaviours and functional competencies which each employee is expected to demonstrate in the performance of the job. These are spelt out in the guidelines and the training materials that support them.

- The system also requires a programme of coaching, mentoring and quarterly progress reviews and annual reviews to rate performance. These skills must be emphasised in the training programmes since they are integral to the programme and it is one of the new features introduced by this system.

- Discussions of career development needs and expectations are also requirements of the system. All quarterly and annual meetings must provide an opportunity not only to identify career expectations but also to work on the development needs of all employees. It ensures that plans are put in place to support these needs so that everything is done to make the employee more effective.

- The recognition of achievement through financial and non-financial awards must be finalised to support this appraisal system. It must also be clear on sanctions, which will follow poor performance. Without this, the system of appraisal becomes as meaningless as the system it replaced.

PILOT STUDY

It was proposed that the system would be implemented in all ministries and departments at the same time, and a period of 9 to 12 months would be used to test it. All training of employees, supervisors and managers would be completed prior to this, and monitoring and continuous training would take place during this period to ensure that the system is properly understood and applied. At the end of the "dry-run", or period of adjustment, the new system would be implemented. It is expected that personnel officers in ministries/departments would play a critical role in the implementation of this phase. In fact, the new system highlights the need for a stronger human resource capacity in organisations to implement and monitor the system properly.

FORMS OF CO-OPERATION

Some departments were most anxious to implement the new system; especially those which had already been seeking to improve on the old system. The training division and the personnel departments readily undertook to train personnel in the use of the system. Individual officers in some departments readily assisted in designing and redesigning the format of the appraisal form until it was as perfect as it could be.

The consultant who had assisted the process had also done a remarkable job in preparing the documentation and the training materials which, when tested through a Training of Trainers' workshop, proved to be excellent.

The Nursing Association, the Police Division, the Civil Aviation Division, the Audit department and the Ministry of Agriculture played key roles in moving the process forward. They gave of their experience and expertise. They shared the information they had garnered in similar exercises and showed a readiness to undertake the new system. Such support is important for other organisations to take the effort seriously.

ANY RESISTANCE TO CHANGE

Agreement has not been reached yet as to whether increments should continue to be automatic or whether they must be achieved through performance. The system proposed that persons who are required to follow a "performance improvement plan" would not receive an increment at the end of the year.

Some personnel thought that the new form was too long and that the strength of the previous one was its brevity. It was also felt that the new system would only improve compliance in the first few years, but would then fall into disuse like others before it.

There were others who thought that the new system would require too much effort, and expressed the view that the new Performance Review and Development System required a high standard of education, probably a university degree, in order to be able to complete the form. This is surely not so, but it does call for a better understanding of the work of the organisation and the role and tasks of the employees in it – something that was not necessary at any time within the old system. It requires some serious work outside the day-to-day activities of the office. As a matter of fact, it places new responsibilities and tasks on staff and this has to be taken into consideration. It is an issue, which teachers emphasised in relation to their own appraisal system to ensure that the new requirements were being factored into their timetables, and adequate allocation of time was being provided.

TRAINING

A massive training programme precedes the implementation of the system. It includes training for a core of trainers from the central training division and ministries/departments; training of all supervisors; and training of all employees. Manuals are provided for each group and each supervisor is expected to attend a two-day seminar while each employee must attend a one-day session. Trainers must cover basic training techniques as well as understand performance management principles, the performance review and development system, its forms and its guidelines. They must recognise the need to develop the new "professionalism" in the public service and be able to assist staff in participating effectively in the processes of the system. They must be able to carry out performance reviews in a fair and unbiased manner and train supervisors and non-supervisors to do the same.

Training for managers and supervisors includes:

- sensitisation to the desired culture for the public service;
- learning how the performance review and development system can contribute to the achievement of that culture;
- understanding of how managers and supervisors will be expected to participate, and how they can assist staff in participating in the process.

In addition, training for non-supervisory employees should allow them to:

- acquire a deeper knowledge of the desired culture of the public service;
- learn how the performance review and development system can assist in the development of this culture;
- become familiar with what the performance review and development system is;
- gain understanding of how non-supervisory employees will be expected to participate;
- become equipped to carry out the processes of the performance review and development system;
- build awareness of how the benefits of the system could be utilised.

Of course, the logistics involved in implementing such a massive training programme for all employees present numerous problems. In the end, it is only the commitment of the trainers, the personnel departments and the employees who will see it through. The time available for training is always going to be a problem and unless managers are keen on the process, the task will indeed be uphill and it may be necessary to begin the programme with departments that are obviously keen on the system.

DIAGNOSIS AND EVALUATION

Review is expected to be an on-going process. However, at the end of the trial period, the Ministry of the Civil Service must diagnose and evaluate the whole process and the returns. Careful analysis will have to be made of the results to determine whether the system has been properly understood and implemented. Immediate action has to be taken to identify what kind of problems have developed and what changes need to be made.

The Ministry of the Civil Service must examine all results to ensure that there has been consistency and that the supervisor/supervisee/management are satisfied with the way the system has worked. Any general inconsistencies must be dealt with decisively. If, for example, a department's results are flawed, they must be rejected and done over again under guidance until they meet the objectives and reinforce the credibility of the new system.

The system must be centrally managed to uphold its integrity and the Ministry of the Civil Service must undertake this task on a regular and on-going basis. It has to ensure that training is maintained for all new entrants to the system and for all new supervisors/managers, and provide refresher courses wherever they are needed. It also must ensure that a relevant training is provided for employees who need to be trained to do their jobs better.

The ministry will also need to ensure that the results are used to improve human resource management in the public service, for not only must they be seen as the basis for promotion, recognition and reward but also for transfers and separation.

The system must be institutionalised to be effective. It must be diagnosed and evaluated at the organisational as well as at the central level. It must be seen as an instrument to improve productivity in the public service and to make Barbados more competitive. It must be seen as an integral part of the Public Sector Reform Programme since it will impact fundamentally on how government does business as long as it remains credible and works towards achieving the objectives that have been set.

REFERENCES

The Laws of Barbados – The Constitution of Barbados

Ministry of the Civil Service – The White Paper on Public Sector Reform in Barbados, 1995

Harris O. Jeff Jnr. – Managing Performance: Cases in Interpersonal Behaviour, pp 277–281. Wiley and Sons Inc.

Charles Polidano, Performance Management in Government: What works, what doesn't. Paper presented in Barbados, October 1999

Keith Davis, Organisational Behaviour and Performance Appraisal, pp 474–479, McGraw-Hill Inc.

Noella Jorm, Julie Hunt, Nick Manning, Working Towards Results, Managing Individual Performance in the Public Service. Commonwealth Secretariat, 1996

David Osbourne and Ted Gaebler, Reinventing Government, pp 138–165, 349–359. Plume

Dorothy M. Stewart, Handbook of Management Skills, 2nd edition, pp 210–222. Gower

NEEDS ANALYSIS AND DESIGN OF PERFORMANCE MANAGEMENT SYSTEMS IN THE SAMOAN PUBLIC SERVICE

Case Study II

Samoa

NEEDS ANALYSIS AND DESIGN OF PERFORMANCE MANAGEMENT SYSTEMS IN THE SAMOAN PUBLIC SERVICE

INTRODUCTION

Samoa is situated just east of the International Dateline making it the last country to say farewell this millennium. Samoa is about 1,770 kilometres north-east of New Zealand and 50 kilometres west of American Samoa. The country consists of two large islands: Upolu (1,100 sq.km.) and Savaii (1,700 sq.km.); and seven smaller islands, two of which, Apolima and Manono, are inhabited. Its total land area is 2,934 sq.km., some 70 per cent of which is arable. The capital Apia is located in Upolu.

Until the early 1890s, Samoa lacked a central political authority over its entire population. Social and political organisation rested largely with the ramified lineage and *aiga* (extended family), and upon the village, where members of several families joined to manage the daily activities of the village. It is the family and the village rather than the individual that are central to the social and political organisation in Samoa. The daily operation of village affairs is vested in the *matais* (chiefs) who constitute the village *fono* (council). The village *fono* comprises chiefs and a *pulenuu* (mayor) responsible for the social and economic welfare of villagers. It also possesses wide powers to discipline *matais*, *aiga* and individuals.

During 1878 and 1879 the United States, Germany and Britain all entered into treaty relations with Samoa. Towards the end of 1899 an agreement was reached to partition the Samoan islands and the United States acquired the eastern islands and the western group of islands was declared a protectorate of Germany. At the outbreak of World War One, the western group of islands under Germany was occupied by New Zealand troops on request from London. In 1946, Western Samoa gained Trusteeship status under the United Nations and in 1962 it attained political independence.

Samoa's population after the 1991 Census stood at 161,298. The total population count as of September 1999 is 169,371. Of this number 88,835 are male and 80,536 are female. About 72 per cent of the total population live on Upolu and 21 per cent of the total population reside in Apia urban area.

According to the World Bank Report (1991), some 100,000 Samoans live overseas, mainly in New Zealand, Australia and mainland America.

The economic conditions for Samoa for the fiscal year 1997/1998 remained positive as Samoa once again registered the highest growth amongst the Pacific island countries. This has followed on from two previous years of outstanding recovery and expansion as the country continued to prosper in the light of more innovative and enabling conditions established by government to foster the development of the private and public sectors.

The total staff establishment for the public service as at 30 June 1998 was 4,264. The number of occupied positions as at the same date was 3,835, a reduction from 3,843 in the previous year. Of this number, females continue to dominate, totalling 2,159, mostly in the teaching and nursing professions, and males numbering 1,676. For the same period, a total of 1,490 casual positions were provided funding in the annual government budget, a decrease of 6% from the previous year's figure of 1,625. Given the Commission's strict monitoring of the level of casual workers, there has been a significant reduction over the years from 2,026 at the end of fiscal year 1992.

The Public Service Commission is empowered under Section 87 of the Constitution of the Independent State of Western Samoa Act 1960 to be responsible for the appointment, promotion, transfer, termination, dismissal and disciplinary control of the Public Service. Within this wide spectrum of HR functions, and related to the issue of performance, the Public Service Commission under the Public Service Act 1977 Section 26 (2), shall grant an annual increment base on the employee's efficiency and conduct thus:

Section 26(2) reads:

> "the right to receive an annual increment shall depend upon the efficiency and conduct of the employee, and shall be determined by the Commission and, if any Permanent Head is of the opinion that an employee should not receive an increment, he shall advise the Commission accordingly, and payment of the increment shall be withheld pending the determination of the Commission as to whether the increment shall be paid."

In compliance with the legislative requirement, the Public Service Commission requires all departments to appraise the performance of all employees occupying established positions within the public service annually, using the existing individual Performance Appraisal Form.

DEVELOPMENT IN THE PUBLIC SERVICE AND DEMANDS FOR BETTER HUMAN RESOURCE PRACTICES

The Appraisal System was instituted way back in the 1970s and has been operational ever since to assess the performance of individual employees and compensate good performers accordingly through the awarding of annual increments. In many cases, developmental purposes associated with having employees' performance appraised, for instance to check on the required skills and experiences or to enable the formulation of strategic management of human resources and training plans, becomes secondary. The appraisal system in place inherits all sorts of problems that will be discussed later in greater detail. But perhaps problems such as the lack of objectivity in assessment and judgement, the validity of factors used across a complex string of positions and position standards, the reliability of ratings by different supervisors, bias, favouritism, and the lack of appreciation and commitment by all parties concerned are either characteristic peculiar to a closely knitted community or are a result of managerial capabilities. Having a workable performance appraisal system is significant and can effectively equip organisations and management in the achievement of excellence on any frontier.

Apart from the array of difficulties embedded in the present system noted above, the other major drawback with the old system is the issue of appropriateness or relevancy to the new public service culture and the demand it places on good performance. During the late 1980s, Cabinet realised that Heads of Departments (HoDs) were as much responsible for the ills in departments' overall performances. This was perceived as a procedural limitation because, although HoDs were responsible to the ministers for the daily management of departments, their appointments were processed and administered by the Public Service Commission. To try and minimise these shortcomings and to instil greater accountability in ministers and greater responsiveness to departmental business, a legislation "Special Posts Act 1989" was passed placing all HoDs on contractual employment. Now Cabinet appoints HoDs for the duration of three years, subject to future amendments. The down side of this initiative is the absence of a corresponding performance management system and a performance agreement between the minister and the head of department of what is expected to be achieved and a tentative timeframe.

To sustain the momentum of public sector reform and the government's belief that the delivery of services and performance can be improved, another initiative was introduced under the financial management reforms by Treasury. On 1 July 1996, government changed its budget format and financial management from a line-item to an output budget system to reinforce better transparency and accountability in service delivery with particular emphasis on improving financial management. Again, like the initiative to place Heads of Departments under contractual employment, an appropriate corresponding incentive system/scheme to reinforce and reward excellent performing departments or a group of workers or individuals was absent. The absence of such a system, whilst the public service has eventually agreed that service is all about good performance, led the Public Service Commission to request assistance from outside expertise through donor assistance. The Commonwealth Secretariat in particular responded, supplying funds for a retreat for Cabinet ministers together with heads of departments and corporations. Moreover, it funded technical assistance to review the existing processes and documentations.

Currently, there are two Performance Appraisal Systems employed by the Public Service Commission to assess individual employees. The old system is still widely used for employees who are not under some sort of contractual employment. This system accounts for more than 95 per cent of total staff establishment in the 26 departments which constitute the public service proper. The newly introduced system is used restrictively for positions on contractual arrangement such as assistant heads of departments and consultant specialists as in professional areas such as medicine and engineering.

THE OLD PERFORMANCE APPRAISAL SYSTEM

The old system is a combination of the Trait and Behaviour-driven system, which essentially assesses the abilities or personal characteristics of an individual employee. The system also tries to measure the extent an employee engages in specific, relatively well-defined behaviour during the performance of his/her duties. As mentioned in the introduction, the old system was designed in the 1970s and as such served its purpose and was suitable for the public service culture then. Now, with so much emphasis on customer services and rapid changes in the public service culture, the old system has become obsolete and does not add any value to the demands of the new culture.

The PSC 4 Annual Personal Report form states eight important factors used by the supervisor to assess employees' performances. Under the "Performance of Duties", an employee will be given a rating of 5 which is the highest score if she/he is "exceptionally efficient. Does more than expected". A rating of 4 means an employee "usually does all that is expected, sometimes more. Usually a quick and efficient worker". An unacceptable behaviour or a rating of 1 is given to an employee whose "output is always below requirement, very slow and inefficient etc.". With the second factor, "Quality of Work" an employee receives a rating of 5 if "consistently does excellent work. Maintains a high standard" and an unacceptable behaviour a rating of 1 under the same factor means an employee "Often makes mistakes. Must always be told to do the job right". Under Factor 7 (Administration), an outstanding rating of 5 means employee "is firm and decisive. Mature judgement. Inspires others. Above criticism". An unacceptable behaviour or a rating of 1 means an employee is "Indecisive. Leans on others. Lacks tact, and commonsense. Tends to irritate others". From these few examples, it is quite clear that the old system and the explanation alongside each of the ratings reflect a supervisor's judgement of employees' traits and behaviour. The old system generally appraises the performance of an individual employee in a rather broad framework instead of specifying achievement or deliverable outputs and outcomes within a given period of time.

The appraisal system is closely connected to the documents used in the selection and recruitment of an employee into the service. These documents are the Detail Form which provides biodata and specifics about an applicant and the other being the Evaluation Form used by the Selection Panel to score each applicant's performance during the interview process. So, in practice, performance appraisal is directly linked to promotion and appointment of officers.

THE REQUIRED PERFORMANCE

The Old System consists of eight (8) factors in which an employee's performance is assessed by the immediate supervisor and submitted to the head of department for its final sanctioning before it goes to the Public Service Commission. The eight factors are:

- Performance of Duties
- Quality of Work
- Knowledge of Work
- Dependability
- Attitude
- Potential for Promotion
- Administration Aptitude
- Relationship with Other Workers

The ranking scale ranges from 1 to 5 with 5 being excellent performance. The definition of each rate is as follows:

- 1 – Unacceptable
- 2 – Unsatisfactory
- 3 – Satisfactory
- 4 – Very Good
- 5 – Outstanding

So far as the Commission is concerned, the required performance of employees should attain an overall average of 3, a lower overall rating demands an explanation from the supervisor and the employee. In some cases, the Commission can rule out a disciplinary decision if the overall rating is very low.

NATURE OF THE PROBLEM

In the present era when personnel performance is so important and as government has introduced performance budgeting, which targets the performance of individual employees closely to the outputs that the public service needs to provide, the prevailing system has become irrelevant and invalid.

The main factors contributing to the limitations of the present system include the following which will be discussed in greater detail below:

- the issue of validity and relevancy to each particular position;
- the issue of reliability and the supervisors' rating;
- the issue of subjectivity, bias and favouritism;
- the issue of consistency in reporting the employee's performance over so many months;
- the issue of commitment and appreciation by the supervisor and the employee that performance appraisal is a crucial management tool in future planning;
- the issue of recognition by management and the employer of the value of performance appraisal and linking it to remuneration and promotion.

The Commission and HoDs, as well as senior managers, are well aware of this potential limitation and have searched for a system which targets performance and output realistically, such as the new one for assistant heads of departments. It is expected that the new system will be mobilised to assess performance for every level of employees in the Samoan public service in the near future.

CONSIDERATION OF CAUSES AND PROBLEM AREAS

a) Validity and relevancy to each particular position

Of the 26 departments that constitute the public service, there are about 90 different professional groups and about 10 clerical or general support services occupational groups. These diverse professions perform unique tasks and activities and therefore require different position standards, skills and competencies. Apart from the extensive differences in position requirements, the performance of tasks of different occupational groups can be achieved better through group or team efforts, or through a few members of that team or individually. In relation to timeliness, achievement of work targets differs amongst employees and positions and at times efficiency is affected by factors beyond an individual's control. These factors include resources, work

129

environment and culture, management approach, organisational practices, systems and processes and other work-related sensitivities.

Generally, some factors might be valid and relevant in the assessment of some employees in some professions but they do not necessarily apply to all employees and to all positions. For example, the work assessment of telecommunication lines and cables technicians, seamen, dentists, doctors and nurses and engineers, to name but a few, should have included risk and stress as important factors rather than administration. Similarly, in the case of junior clerical staff, their daily position requirements are basically routine whereas policy analysts and researchers require much more advanced competencies and their work is much more complicated and demanding in relation to meeting datelines.

b) Reliability and supervisors' ratings

Real case scenarios demonstrate this problem. Within one of the large departments in one particular division, a mature supervisor who had served in the department for more than 20 years, normally appraised her immediate subordinate staff on an average of either 4.5 or 5. These ratings were for 1996 and 1997. When supervisor A passed away and a new supervisor was appointed, the same immediate staff received ratings of either 3.7 or 3.8 for their performance appraisal reports in 1998.

In many cases, supervisors would consistently rate their subordinate staff '5' in every single factor, as such employees have consistently shown outstanding performances on the basis of the assessment scale. However, the same employees could be warned and charged for negligence or insubordination or for embezzlement of government funds during the same period they consistently received ratings of '5'.

The cases in hand obviously reflect that different supervisors rate employees differently and that factors in the appraisal form are weighted different by supervisors depending on their opinions of the position. Otherwise, supervisors feel that employees should be given higher ratings until their performances are obviously unacceptable or unsatisfactory.

130

The current performance appraisal system is further hindered in its effectiveness because of subjective judgement, bias and favouritism which are supposedly not confined to the public service, but examples of which are much more intrinsic because it is a closely knit community and therefore the tendency for supervisors to give chances for employees to improve when circumstances warrant a disciplinary action.

Within one department, where most senior positions are occupied by professional employees, it is common knowledge amongst the senior management level of departments working closely with this particular department that the HoD displays absolute favouritism and bias towards professional employees who are in the third and fourth levels of the organisation rather than those immediately in the second level. The HoD's unprofessional behaviour towards the immediate subordinates includes the indirect exclusion of them from policy decisions and staff-related matters which fundamentally impact on divisional work plan allocation. This sort of behaviour, to a certain degree, affects the performance and working morale of those senior officers in the second level and results in a lack of support, trust and confidence in the HoD.

On the other hand, those preferred employees capitalise on the opportunities available and because their standing needs and professional demands are usually satisfied, correspondingly their performances excel at the cost of a broad organisational effectiveness and harmony. Within this particular department, the senior officers openly criticise the HoD's poor management approach and absence of people's skills. As an outsider looking in, the behaviour of the HoD has to do with low self-esteem and an inferiority complex that senior officers are so competent and extrovert and therefore sees it as potential threat.

In another department, the HoD who is a specialist by training is seen generally by employees as a weak leader who tends to depend heavily on the head of Corporate Services. This inclination derives from the HoD's lack of management/ administration experience and knowledge. In return, the head of Corporate Services cultivates the HoD's dependency because it consolidates the Corporate Services influence on other Divisional Heads. Apart from the influence and preferential admission this symbiotic relationship exerts on other Divisional Heads, there is a comparative advantage this working relationship cultivates to improve the profile and status of the Corporate Services, not to mention the unnecessary anxiety on the employees. In fact, since there are several other similar instances, one questions the capability of specialists becoming administrators or managers, especially in view of the absence in people skills.

Nepotism is not uncommon but the willingness of employees to report the matter to the Public Service Commission is often hindered by Samoan values and beliefs such as respect and obedience as well as the Christian principle of forgiveness. Recently, a school-leaver wrote a letter complaining about the recruitment practice used by one core department whereby the school-leaver claimed that sons and daughters of Methodist Church Ministers were given preference. The complaint had some truth in it with regard to the hiring of casual workers but, unfortunately, the incumbent HoD acquired the problem from the former HoD. The hiring of casual workers was delegated by the Commission to HoDs and, in this case, those currently holding junior clerical positions enter government service as casual workers and, because of their familiarities with the tasks involved, subsequently had a better chance of filling an existing vacancy ahead of an outsider.

Another contributing factor to the subjective assessment by supervisors rests with the *matai* system. There are known cases where supervisors have rated their subordinate staff who are *matais* much higher than they actually deserve out of respect. One needs to reflect on the social organisation in the Samoan context to understand this fully. The practice is more evident in positions where the subordinate assume the duties of the supervisor, such as meeting with the community, and largely because the situation requires a *matai* to handle the situation. Inevitably, an assessment of the subordinate in carrying out his/her actual duties is compromised because he/she is doing the supervisor a favour.

There are numerous real cases where supervisors including HoDs favour or display a degree of bias towards employees they like or who think and work like them. This limitation is perhaps inevitable even in the most well-defined performance management system because supervisors' weaknesses, as well as employees, are a aprt of human nature.

CONSISTENCY IN REPORTING EMPLOYEES' PERFORMANCES

Apart from the system's inherited weaknesses, a more disturbing management limitation to performance appraisal stems from supervisors' poor record-keeping and frequent reporting on employees' performance. It is common in the Samoan context that the bulk of supervisors will only prepare an employee's performance appraisal report just before the due date. This practice is perhaps related to the supervisors' management approach and the absence of weekly or fortnightly management meetings where departmental and divisional targets are not followed up and supervisors therefore miss the broad positioning of employees' achievements within a certain timeframe.

A few years back, a stenographic secretary in a central department was asked to resign when the management had exhausted all disciplinary measures available to refrain her from using office phone for personal overseas calls. In the submission to the Commission which led to the termination of her services, offences committed by this employee were listed, yet her annual reports for the same period were rated as outstanding or averaged at 4.8 or 5.

What can be seen from this scenario is the supervisor's lack of consistency, honesty and integrity for scoring the stenographer's performance as outstanding for four consecutive years whilst simultaneously ignoring her continuous displays of dishonesty, insubordination and negligence. One also questions the capability of the supervisor to remain in that position. In fact, the unauthorised usage of office phone for personal overseas calls was finally used to terminate her service when the bottom line was that her performance was anything but unsatisfactory.

COMMITMENT AND APPRECIATION BY ALL PARTIES THAT PERFORMANCE APPRAISAL IS A MANAGEMENT TOOL

Again, similar to the above example, the lack of commitment and appreciation by those involved in the real problems and hindrances to any performance appraisal report has little to do with the system but rather the people who implement the system.

As explained earlier, the main purpose for the submission of personal appraisal reports is to satisfy the legislation so that employees can receive their annual increments. On that basis, the commitment expected both from supervisors and the subordinate staff to carry out this exercise with the utmost sincerity is often overlooked. It is not unusual to hear and observe supervisors and employees alike sitting down together for less than five minutes and predetermining a scoring for a particular year without doing a proper analysis of the employee's actual performance. Such occurrences mean that employees' weaknesses and, therefore the necessity to acquire specific skills to achieve set organisational tasks and goals, are not tackled.

On the other hand, there have been cases where supervisors provide realistic assessments of employees' performances as unreliable and requiring vast improvement in specific areas. Since the employees do not want negative performance appraisal reports which provide a true account of their performances they refuse to sign. In some cases, they can resort to taking their grievances to the HoDs and the Commission, appealing for a fair hearing and seeking a second chance from higher authorities.

Generally, the preparation of performance appraisal reports is often seen by supervisors as a time-wasting exercise. On the other hand, most employees see it as a way for the supervisors to belittle their abilities or as a mean of settling any differences of opinion with the supervisor holding the upper hand. In many cases. both supervisors and employees fulfil the task because of the fact that employees will receive annual increments at the end of a satisfactory year.

RECOGNITION AND LINKING IT TO REMUNERATION AND PROMOTION

Prior to the introduction of performance budget, performance appraisals were linked directly to remuneration. The process had significant recognition in that respect. Since the suspension of annual increments in 1995 the recognition usually accorded to annual performance appraisal reports diminished to the extent that many employees do not have performance appraisal reports since 1996. The legislated preparation and provision of individual performance appraisal reports is linked closely to promotion and its absence indicates the absolute lack of commitment by supervisors and employees to the whole process. In a case where two applicants are equally qualified for a vacant position, the applicant with progressive performance appraisal reports has a better chance of getting the job.

Having served in the public service under the old performance appraisal system, the following observation by Mr Alex Matheson, a former advisor from the Commonwealth Secretariat who assisted our efforts to revamp the prevailing system, reflects the truism expressed above:

> *"...the system itself is not designed in a way that encourages managers to take an active and responsible approach to their managerial responsibilities and it could lead to some managers focusing excessively on their personal or political interests, and neglecting to give staff support and direction, and making uniformed and unfair judgements about them – or failing to attend to their performance at all. It could also lead to some staff, in the absence of direction and with little inducement or encouragement to perform well, giving their attention to matters other than their main duties, and thus contribute to bureaucratic, risk averse and time serving behaviour."*

OVERVIEW OF THE OLD PERFORMANCE APPRAISAL SYSTEM

The conflict, seen in the Samoan context, between the old and the new system stems from employees' reluctance to change their old working habits/attitudes and behaviour as required by the imposed changes. For instance, when the new performance budget was introduced in 1996, managers were required to prepare their budgets on the basis of departmental deliverable outputs. The format for budget preparations had been explained to departments through many workshops conducted by the Treasury Department. Interestingly, at the budget-screening three years later, a significant number of HoDs and senior officers were still talking about inputs rather than outputs. In relation to performance appraisal, HoDs and supervisors alike find it hard to even assess employees' performances against the achievement or otherwise of stated outputs. In fact, more than 80 per cent of total public servants had no performance appraisal reports since the first year of performance budgeting for the following reasons:

135

a) A freeze was placed on increments for public servants because of the financial constraints experienced by the country's national carrier, together with the taro leaf blight;

b) Simultaneously, there was zero commitment by everyone involved, although appraisal reports of employees are part of managerial responsibility and are essential to employees' promotion and training plans; and

c) There should have been a new performance system corresponding to the new budget framework if the emphasis was on outputs rather than inputs.

At the macro-level, the decision by Cabinet to contract HoDs relates to the carefree and non-committal attitude displayed by HoDs to Cabinet ministers. Prior to 1990, HoDs were appointed by the Commission like any other public servant. Since the positions were contractual, Cabinet does the selection whilst the Commission administers the recruitment process. A former Cabinet minister who likes to tell tales of his ministerial times explained how he warned several HoDs under the various portfolios he held for their obvious display of insubordination and the carefree attitude to implement Cabinet directives. One of these HoDs had his contract terminated when the same minister was still in Cabinet. Now wearing a different hat as a Commission member, he firmly believes that HoDs should remain on contract and continue to be appointed by Cabinet.

POTENTIAL CAUSES OF THE PROBLEM

- Cumbersome bureaucratic procedures, systems and structures;
- Lack of understanding by all involved because of the absence of proper induction training on the area of staff appraisal;
- Samoan values and beliefs – supervisors who are *non-matais* still need to treat subordinates who are *matais* with a lot of respect;
- Lack of commitment, sincerity and professionalism by supervisors when assessing employees' performances because of family connections and friendships etc;
- Lack of follow-up action on the necessity of appraisal reports and the implementation of their outcomes by the HoDs and the Commission;

- Lack of initiative by employees to remind supervisors when their performance appraisal reports are due; and
- It is a time-consuming exercise, especially on the part of the supervisor.

IDENTIFYING THE TASKS THAT WERE NOT BEING PERFORMED

Generally, since the appreciation and commitment by all parties concerned (Commission, HoDs, supervisors and employees) with the preparation and review of performance appraisal reports was paid mere lip service, the following tasks were inadequately performed:

a) The comprehensive analysis of skills required by employees was not done professionally and as a result, huge investment in terms of resources and time allocated for training and development was lost. In other words, the nomination of employees to participate in short-term training programmes primarily to improve their knowledge, skills and attitudes had been rather *ad hoc* in nature and unsystematic, resulting in the wrong employees attending training. A much worse case scenario is the perception by many supervisors and employees alike that participation in training programmes is a reward for being efficient, however, effectively loosing the real value of training.

b) That incomprehensive performance appraisal of employees, particularly in cases of overrating, could very well result in promoting the wrong person to positions of responsibility. We have seen a lot of cases where employees have been promoted to positions beyond their competencies and know-how and the situation is unpleasant for the employee, the organisation and the Commission. Given the interrelatedness among individual appraisal system, selection and recruitment and promotion, a lot is at stake because of poor performance appraisal.

c) In many cases, one of the tasks totally overlooked by supervisors is the frequent/consistent notation of employees' performances. This results in inadequate appraisal and therefore the tendency to just complete forms rather than having a meaningful consultation between supervisors and employees. In fact, there have been cases where employees have challenged supervisors' assessments of their performances and, in some instances, the Commission has had to mediate to resolve departmental disputes.

d) The non-production of annual employees' appraisal reports is a real legal issue now, and even the Commission can contest in court the irresponsibility of HoDs, supervisors and employees.

THE INTRODUCTION OF A NEW PERFORMANCE MANAGEMENT SYSTEM

The new public service culture is about efficiency and effectiveness as well as "talking and walking" the principles of good governance such as being fair, transparent, accountable, predictable, consultative etc. Subsequently, the new public service culture is more concerned with quality service to customers and clients at a reasonable cost and timeliness. Gone are the habits of clients having to wait while public servants take their time and have no regard for customers. Public servants who have served for many years under the old system find it difficult to adjust to the paradigm shift which places priority and importance on customers and clients. Under the old system, employees focus on serving their interests and that of the organisation. In other words, the performance of the public service now is being assessed openly by the public much more than the closed, confidential and secretive system of the Sixties, Seventies and early-Eighties. Such a culture remained one of a widely used management text during the Eighties, something along the lines of 'public money and private government'.

The Commission is well aware of the present system's limitations and has decided to design a system that corresponds with performance budgeting and a system that reinforces the accountability of public servants to the outputs or services to be delivered. It is also the intention of the Commission that, with the devolution of most personnel functions to line departments, HoDs should be made responsible for managing of staff performance. In late 1998, with the amendment to Section 55 of the Public Service Act 1977, the second level, or assistant directors/secretaries, were place on contractual employment together with performance agreements to consolidate a performance-based culture in departments. The decision by the Commission to contract the second level means that a proper contract document is required, as well as a performance agreement document, if the objective of the decision is to be realistically realised. The main rationale behind this decision is to reward only excellent performers and to weave out the non-performers. Such a solution goes hand in hand with the objectives of the performance budget as assistant directors and secretaries take on more responsibilities as output managers. On a purely HR policy matter, such a decision allows for quicker promotions for those able, innovative and risk-taking managers who, in real terms, are the catalysts for a changing public service culture.

THE CONSULTATION PROCESS

Having agreed to place the second level on contract, the Commission did not readily agree to the idea of consultation with HoDs and the assistant HoDs. The preferred approach by the Commission was very much a top-down implementation and to tell both parties about the Commission decision. Nevertheless, having thought of best practices in countries which have done this, in addition to the fact that in the real Samoan way, a decision of such importance and magnitude requires extensive consultation with those involved. This is based on the understanding that if people understand they will support the decision. On that realisation, a Committee of four was established comprising the Chairman of the Public Accounts Committee of Parliament, the Financial Secretary, the Controller and Chief Auditor and the Secretary Public Service Commission.

The Committee familiarised themselves with the tasks in hand and in particular with the content of both the contract document and the performance agreement document. Afterwards, the work of the Committee was to explain and discuss with HoDs the Commission's intention and an opportunity was given for comments. In view of the large number, HoDs were called in in groups of four or five. Most HoDs agreed with the new arrangement but their concerns had to do with the time of performance review. Some agreed to a six- monthly review, others argued for an annual review and several thought that quarterly reviews were more appropriate. Other comments were related to who had the authority on the contract, the HoD or the Commission. Other comments were directed at the content of both documents. These consultations took two whole days and the Committee then sanctioned comments put forward for their inclusion or otherwise in the final copy of the contract and performance agreement documents.

The second round of consultations was with all assistants, and several small departments were dealt with together whilst bigger departments were consulted independently. Within 26 departments, including the Public Service Commission, there are about 90 assistants. The second round of consultations was between the assistants and the Secretary PSC, an assistant HRM/OC and the Head of the Legal Unit of the PSC. The participation of these two senior officers of the Commission office was essential to assist in the explanation of technical elements of the contract.

The outcome of this round of consultation was much more intensive in terms of the feedback from assistants. The main concerns were the conditions of employment in terms of salaries and allowances, duration of contract and leave entitlements. They argued that their package should be closely related to that offered to HoDs. The most interesting comment was their mistrust of HoDs' neutrality and fairness and therefore their insistence that the contract should be between them and the Commission and the HoD could be party to it. The point is valid and legally HoDs cannot be the main partner or exercise the role of the employer which is constitutionally vested in the Commission. The signature and endorsement of HoDs is still necessary so that there is a formal agreement between them and the assistants to achieve specific outputs within a financial year.

There was very little resistance from the assistants, basically because they were given a much better employment package in terms of salaries, allowances and leave conditions compared to the employment as mere public servants. Furthermore, those who work hard and are committed to performance will be given bonuses at the end of the financial year. This bonus system is still being negotiated between the Treasury and the Commission. Similarly, most young assistants see this decision as a chance to greater mobility up and between departments as all positions will be advertised at the completion of the second year.

The involvement of the staff association was rather indirect but was encouraged by the Commission. Like any other occasion in the Samoan context, conflicts and resistance were resolved through effective consultations and better understanding of the issues. As with this case, the Samoan consultative approach as well as cultural values and beliefs, such as respect of and obedience to those in positions of authority, played a significant role in dispelling any negative feelings.

The process contributes to the reform programme of government by consolidating the following factors:

a) That employment tenure in the government service is no longer protected from public scrutiny and therefore the retention of an officer based on long service and until one reaches retiring age can no longer be gauranteed.

b) That placing HoDs and assistants on contractual employment encourages the performance culture much needed within the government service so that we care for clients and customers, as well as ensuring the delivery of timely, cost-effective and quality services.

The long-term implication of this decision if ministers, the Commission and HoDs are sincere about performance reviews, is the need to really rethink the necessity of the current number of departments and their division of work. This assumption is largely based on skills scarcity in many professional areas, including managerial skills. A reduction in the number of departments would greatly enhance the service as the small pool of much-needed professionals such as IT, accountants and policy analysts generally will be available. Currently, with the existence of 26 departments, each is competing for good and capable accountants, IT personnel and the like, not to mention the competition with the private sector.

What follows highlights the basic components of a contemporary performance management system devised for the second level and which has since been adapted to be also used for the Heads of Departments. It is expected that the middle management level of the public service will adopt a similar performance management system. The new system is intended to arrest and minimise the known limitations of the old system.

BASIC COMPONENTS OF THE NEW PERFORMANCE AGREEMENT DOCUMENT

As mentioned earlier on, the Commission's intention in devising a new performance management system is to consolidate the gains already achieved in the financial management reform programmes co-ordinated by the Treasury Department. The new form allows a lot more flexibility for both the supervisor and the employee to discuss and come to an agreement creating a much more trusting work environment.

Key areas of responsibility

The identification of key areas of responsibility is a share activity between the department's senior management and the Public Service Commission at the determination whether a position is to become an established position???. Since most of the second level positions are established senior positions, their advertisements are still subject to the Commission's sanctioning of position standards and requirements in terms of skills, behaviour and competencies. The key areas of responsibilities should be closely linked to government's broad development objectives, sectoral plans, departmental corporate plan, budget outputs and the description of the position. In view of the fact that it is tied to the budget programme, the targeted timeframe should be linked to the budget.

Consultative review process assessing employees' skills

This component consists of Personal Skills, Professional/Technical Skills, People Skills, Resource Management Skills and Management Skills with sub-categorisation to enable the employee and the supervisor to rate the employee's capability in achieving the work targets or aims. Unlike the old system where the employee is given no room to make a self-appraisal, this new system provides that opportunity. It was also the intention of the Public Service Commission that any unresolved conflict in views can be settled during this meeting.

Personal Development Plan

In view of the rapid changes affecting the public service today and the general views of prominent psychologists that individuals know better their development needs, it is only fair that they should be given the opportunity to conduct this assessment. It is also beneficial to the supervisor and the department to know employees' aspirations in terms of their future careers and to provide a facilitating role in order to maximise employees' strengths.

The emphasis placed on this component of the new performance assessment document allows the employee to assess and match his/her existing skills to the skills required by the organisation so that the position achieves its goals. For instance, the job description ought to state clearly what is required to be done within a required timeframe and in relation to the overall function or goals of the department. Within the job description, the required qualification is usually included in the advertisement as well as the skills required in relation to people, communication and computing. Where there is difficulty in recruiting the right person, as is the case in specialised fields, the department will still recruit the best candidate out of the applicants and train him/her. This is provided the applicant is willing and has the potential to learn.

As such, the personal development plan is essential and employees ought to be honest about their inadequacies so that the supervisor can request specific training to address any skills gap. This is a common occurrence in the Samoan public service as departments take on new responsibilities agreed to by government such as a world convention, i.e. WTO and environment-related conventions or good governance and human rights conventions. In some cases, departments propose a project to strengthen its service and the last factor HoDs think about during the planning phase is people with the required skills to carry out the project.

Training Needs Identification

Again, unlike the old system, the new system requires the employee to state the skills he/she lacks, however essential in the daily performance of agreed aims and work plans. This exercise should also include skills required in the future in view of the employee's personal development plan and the future needs of the department. Although this is identified primarily by the employee, it is within the interest of the supervisor to double-check this during the performance review meeting.

Apart from the flexibility built into the new performance appraisal system allowing initially the employee to identify his/her training needs, there is a formal system operative in the government service. HoDs and supervisors ought to work together in the identification of training needs of employees. Similar to the personal development plan, HoDs and supervisors, through fortnightly management meetings, should discuss the performance of each division and employees, identify goals that are inadequately performed and tease out the skills gap of existing employees. If such a task is performed rigorously and systematically then the organisation would be in a better position to target training programmes for those employees who require their skills to be upgraded. Usually this process is often addressed through the provision of short-term training programmes, either overseas at some institutes in donor countries or locally with facilitators recruited from donor countries.

Several training policies and strategies are in place for the government service:

a) The in-country training programme mainly targets a large number of requests both from the public and private sectors which require knowledge and skills in general administrative-related activities. Over the years, the in-country training programme has included specialised areas and private sector initiatives relating mainly to the establishment of small businesses and income-generating projects, for instance landscaping, flower arrangement, orchid propagation and tissue culture, packing and marketing etc. At present, three donors are actively involved in the in-country training programme: New Zealand, Australia and the Hann Siedel Foundation (Germany). The Public Service Commission plays the co-ordinating role while the administrative activities have now been delegated to the requesting agency to manage the programme. The host/requesting agency has the final clearance whether to accept the facilitator selected by the donor country.

b) Overseas short-term training is offered by donor countries or institutes and the participation of employees is initially identified and sanctioned by the HoD and the request is put to the Staff Training and Scholarship Committee. This Committee is chaired by the Minister of Education and the Committee also handles all long-term training or the scholarship scheme.

c) The long-term training policy objective is to address areas of skills shortage for national development. Prior to 1996, the emphasis of the long-term training policy was on the government service, however, with the government's partnership with the private sector, training needs and opportunities should be considered nationally. In this regard, the role of the Labour Department in synthesising skills requirements at the national level is pivotal. The Public Service Commission continues to advise the Staff Training and Scholarship Committee on requirements within the government services.

Agreed aims to work on and improve

Whereas in the Key Areas of Responsibility the general scope of the position is provided, agreed aims to work on and improve focus specifically on some outputs of the division/department. Every aim or goal must be completed within a specific time-frame. Again like the other components, the employee has a greater flexibility to influence the outcome of the position.

During the review phase, the employee is given a chance to rate his/her own performance according to the scale of 1–5 as set out in the document. The supervisor is supposed to perform the same task afterwards. In the event that there is a significant difference in ratings, the employee and the supervisor discuss and look at ways to improve that area in the future. Where a conflict of views arises, the matter will then be referred to the Commission.

IMPLEMENTING THE NEW PERFORMANCE APPRAISAL

Essentially, the underpinning principle built into this new performance appraisal system is to encourage transparency and accountability amongst all parties, the employee, supervisor and the department, so that the overall vision of a better Samoa can be achieved as efficiently and effectively as possible.

The new system was implemented in October 1998. At the completion of the extensive consultation processes discussed above, it was the general opinion that the new system could be implemented. Like any new initiative, there will be modification later as proposed by both Matheson and Jorm, but it was generally felt that amendments to the existing document immediately were immature. It was also agreed to wait until the first anniversary of the contract is completed and the first performance reviews submitted before making amendments.

The benefits of the new performance review system is that everyone involved is in a win-win situation and Matheson (1999) has highlighted these advantages for the supervisor/manager, the employee and for both. The various aspects of performance prescribed by Matheson as follows can be adopted to improve our Performance Review Document thus:

- Output/Services and Projects;
- Building Capacity of Staff and Institutions;
- Output Appropriation and Performance Agreements;
- Corporate Requirements and Contributions;
- Key Results.

ASPECTS OF PERFORMANCE

Output/Services and Projects

According to Matheson, one cannot classify all public service positions as similar and therefore any performance review system needs to be flexible to reflect the complexities and differences. The differentiation provided in this case is between output/services-oriented sorts of positions which are project-based. According to Matheson, service or output-related jobs "have quite specific but broadly applicable performance criteria or standards". In the case of project-related jobs, there are "generic quality criteria", i.e. timeliness but the assessment should be measured against the achievement of project objectives.

Building Capacity of Staff and Institutions

The argument here is that organisations should continue to prepare through training and development programmes the capacity of individual and institutions to cope with future demands. The capacity building for institutions is not confined to human resources but to policies, systems and processes.

Output Appropriation and Performance Agreements

The importance of outputs appropriation is closely related to the performance of the two top levels of the organisation which are now on contractual employment. According to Matheson, the outputs do not necessarily specify performance or are used to assess performance. Once again the separation between services and projects activities must be specified for effective assessment.

Corporate Requirements and Contributions

The assessment and recording of staff performance should not be strictly confined to the division of specific tasks because of the truism in the public service that employees do a lot more than their prescribed tasks.

Key Results

The much more complicated public service jobs carry out extra as directed and such performance should also be taken into account. Key results are measurable because they must be completed within a specified timeframe and resources, and the achievement of such should be reported.

To strengthen our Performance Review format, the proposal by Matheson on the inclusion of specific elements so that departments can utilise it flexibly to meet the needs of various occupational groups includes the following:

- Position Title
- Job Description
- Key Results
- Outputs or Services
- Projects/Activities Divided
- Personal Development Plan
- Training Needs
- Comments and Amendments
- Assessment

As mentioned before, the design of a workable performance management system should incorporate the national vision, sectoral plan, departmental corporate plan and the budget process and although the following flow diagram by Noella Jorm (1999) is adapted for its user-friendliness, the inclusion of sectoral plans must be integrated and acknowledged as their presence allows better alignment of departmental corporate plans.

The proposal to incorporate all layers of the planning cycle is fundamentally critical because they are all interrelated. The government's Statement of Economic Strategy clearly set out the vision which it will try and achieve within the two-year period. Sectoral plans refer to different sectors but emphasis is placed on priority sectors such as education, health, agriculture and tourism. Their purpose is to provide goals which each government service department can relate to in the daily provision of deliverables. It also helps departments to focus their operations on core business and functions which do comply with the sector development objectives. Having sector plans assists departments with the production of corporate plans and budget preparation. The whole process in short, is to verify the necessity of resources given to departments for the delivery of quality, cost-effective and timely services to the public.

Performance Management Principles and Benefits

The Performance Management processes ensure that government's vision and goals are translated into planning and achieved through the agreements and actions of individuals.

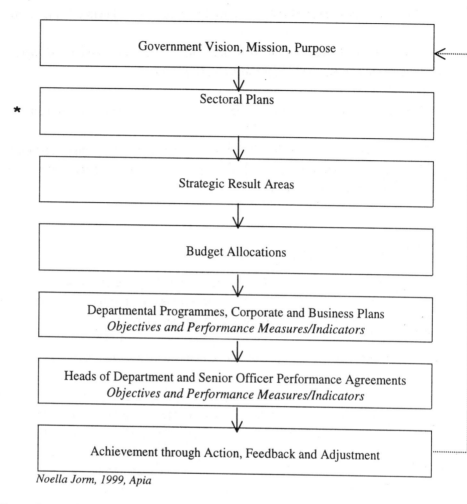

```
┌─────────────────────────────────────────────────┐
│         Government Vision, Mission, Purpose       │ ◄┄┄┄┄┐
└─────────────────────────────────────────────────┘      ┆
                        │                                  ┆
                        ▼                                  ┆
┌─────────────────────────────────────────────────┐      ┆
★│                   Sectoral Plans                  │      ┆
└─────────────────────────────────────────────────┘      ┆
                        │                                  ┆
                        ▼                                  ┆
┌─────────────────────────────────────────────────┐      ┆
│                Strategic Result Areas             │      ┆
└─────────────────────────────────────────────────┘      ┆
                        │                                  ┆
                        ▼                                  ┆
┌─────────────────────────────────────────────────┐      ┆
│                 Budget Allocations                │      ┆
└─────────────────────────────────────────────────┘      ┆
                        │                                  ┆
                        ▼                                  ┆
┌─────────────────────────────────────────────────┐      ┆
│   Departmental Programmes, Corporate and Business Plans │ ┆
│   Objectives and Performance Measures/Indicators  │      ┆
└─────────────────────────────────────────────────┘      ┆
                        │                                  ┆
                        ▼                                  ┆
┌─────────────────────────────────────────────────┐      ┆
│ Heads of Department and Senior Officer Performance Agreements │ ┆
│   Objectives and Performance Measures/Indicators  │      ┆
└─────────────────────────────────────────────────┘      ┆
                        │                                  ┆
                        ▼                                  ┆
┌─────────────────────────────────────────────────┐      ┆
│   Achievement through Action, Feedback and Adjustment │ ┄┄┘
└─────────────────────────────────────────────────┘
```

Noella Jorm, 1999, Apia

Note: Sectoral Plan has been added to Ms Jorm's flowchart because it does have a place in the Samoan planning context.

The performance management processes aim to develop a performance culture in Samoa where:

- The task of each department and individual is linked to the achievement of the goals of Government;

- Heads of Department and Senior Officers have the opportunity to discuss, agree and receive feedback on the tasks and performance measures/indicators they are expected to achieve;

- A clear guidance standard of required management behaviour is provided;

- Reward and recognition outcomes are based on review of agreed performance measures/indicators and standards;

- Skills and career development needs of officers are identified and met;

- Confidentiality of review processes, provision of dispute resolution mechanisms and provisions of training in performance management act to ensure fairness and equity.

CONCLUSION

The initiative should be credited in the search to professionalise the public sector leaps forward, together with the provision of more autonomy and flexibility for the manager to manage its human resource.

To institutionalise the new performance management system successfully, the Commission needs to package the process so that it is marketable and that Heads of Department, assistants and the whole middle-management level should participate in a training programme to ensure the successful implementation and monitoring of the system. Heads of Department should be given the flexibility to tailor some aspects of the performance management form to suit their needs. Performance Management should be an integral part of managers' and employees' annual planning cycle and the process should be linked directly to personal development, further training, promotion and financial recognition for its sustainability.

It is also recommended that the performance review process should involve the following:
- at least two formal reviews a year;
- a minimum of six monthly review;
- an annual assessment;
- mutual managerial/employee sign-off of objectives;
- written representation of performance by employee;
- verification of performance, and independent monitoring information by manager; and

- setting minimum standards for review meetings.

(Matheson, 1999, p. 9)

REFERENCES

Jorm, Noella (1999). *Guide to Performance Agreement: For Head of Department and Senior Officers*, Apia

Matheson, Alex (1999). *Proposed Performance Management System for the Public Service of Samoa*, Apia

Government of Samoa Publications:

- Strengthening the Partnership: A Statement of Economic Strategy, 1998–1999, Treasury Dept, Samoa, March 1999
- Western Samoa Statutes Reprint (1996), *PSC Act 1977*. Office of the Legislative, Samoa
- Western Samoa Statutes Reprint (1996). *Special Post Act 1989*. Office of the Legislative, Samoa
- Budget Documents
- PSC presentation at the Retreat on Directing and Managing Performance, Feb 1999, Kitano Tusitala, Apia

CASE STUDY III

TONGA

INTRODUCTION

The Government of Tonga, as part of its vision for national development, is committed to the creation and maintenance of an efficient and well-structured government sector, which embodies the qualities of good governance and accountability.

In order to help achieve both the national vision and a more effective government sector, a strategic planning framework has been developed. Ministries and departments identify, on an on-going basis, the programmes and outputs required. The Tonga Civil Service Performance Management System links the tasks and performance of job-holders throughout the civil service to support the achievement of the government's desired outcomes.

The Strategic Planning and Performance Management Framework

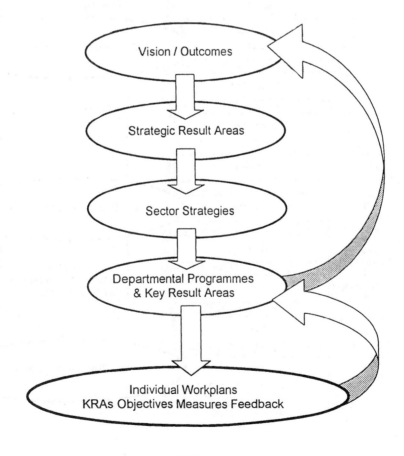

PURPOSE OF THE TONGA CIVIL SERVICE PERFORMANCE MANAGEMENT SYSTEM

The purpose of the system is to ensure that individual effort is linked to government objectives and job-holders are provided with the clear roles and goals, coaching, feedback and appropriate reward and development to sustain a culture of continuous performance improvement.

How the Performance Management Appraisal System Works

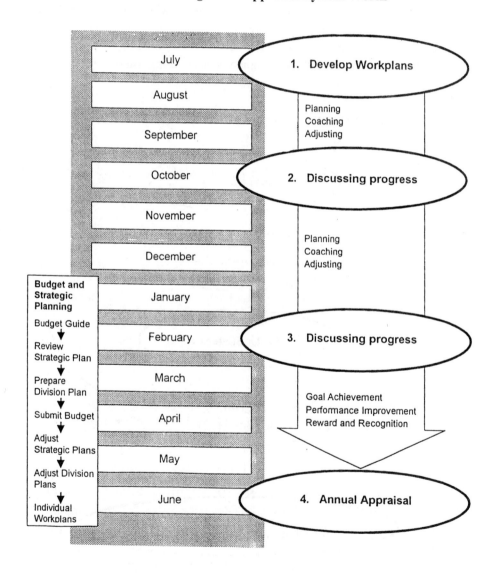

1. Each July or when a job-holder starts in a department

Appraiser and job-holder prepare the performance work plan and discuss the expected behaviours of the Tonga Capability Standard. They develop objectives and performance measures/outputs in line with the department's objectives and the job-holder's position description. Objectives cover the total job functions and are specific, measurable, realistic and time-framed. Where a number of job-holders carry out the same function, they have objectives and measures in common. Appraiser and job-holder agree on any additional skills acquisition required for expected completion of objectives and record this on the work plan.

The appraiser and the job-holder each hold a copy of the Performance Management Appraisal Form.

2. During the appraisal year on an on-going basis

Appraiser and job-holder discuss progress, participate in coaching and feedback, and work together to resolve problems as they arise.

3. In October and February

Appraiser and job-holder have a formal progress meeting. They record any changes to the work plan, or agreements made for early resolution of performance difficulties.

The appraiser forwards recommendations relating to probation to the Establishments Division.

4. At the end of the appraisal year (June), or the end of probationary period, or on promotion or transfer

Appraiser and job-holder meet to discuss the year's progress and to rate how well the job-holder has achieved objectives and demonstrated the Tonga Capability Standard behaviours. They also discuss the appraiser's recommendations in relation to performance recognition or unsatisfactory performance. Career development is also discussed. If the job-holder's performance is below standard, a performance improvement agreement is developed. The job-holder and the appraiser then provide comments and sign off the appraisal form.

The next level managers oversight the completed appraisals for their area, resolve any disagreements or discrepancies and confirm performance recognition and dealing with unsatisfactory performance recommendations.

Appraisals are forwarded to the Establishments Division for implementing with performance recognition recommendations. The Performance Appraisal form is lodged on the job-holder's confidential personnel file.

PARTICIPANTS IN THE PERFORMANCE MANAGEMENT APPRAISAL

The Performance Management Appraisal System will cover every member of the Tonga Civil Service except Heads of Department. Systems for the appraisal of Heads of Department are being researched.

Those covered include employees, supervisors and senior managers from all departments, job-holders on probation and temporary employees.

Civil Service employees (job-holders) develop their work-plan with their supervisor or manager (their appraiser). They receive coaching, assistance and continuous feedback throughout the year and participate in an open, objective appraisal at the end of each year.

Training is provided for every job-holder before they commence participation in the Performance Management Appraisal System.

Tonga Civil Service Performance Management System Appraisal forms and guides, together with advice and support on participation in the system, are available from the Establishments Division, Government Headquarters.

THE ROLE JOB-HOLDERS PLAY

Job-holders:

- Develop draft objectives and measures for discussion with their appraiser during their work plan development meeting each January or when they start in a new position.

- Consider if they need additional skills to complete their objectives and discuss these with their appraiser.

- Finalise the work plan for signing after they and their appraiser agree on the contents.

- Raise with their appraiser any changes they believe should be made to their objectives or performance measures/outputs during progress meetings.

- Prepare for the annual appraisal meeting by considering how well output requirements and the Tonga Capability Standard have been met.

- Bring forward their achievements and discuss performance and their future career in an open manner during appraisal meetings.

THE ROLE APPRAISERS PLAY

Appraisers:

- Conduct a unit meeting where the objectives of the unit, in line with departmental priorities, individual roles and responsibilities and any objectives and outputs that are common to a number of unit job-holders, are discussed and agreed.

- Conduct an annual work plan development meeting with each job-holder.

- Ensure that notice is given and time put aside for work plan development progress and annual appraisal meetings to be conducted in a confidential and supportive manner.

- During the performance management meetings, focus on positive solutions and strategies for performance improvement.

- If performance problems in relation to objectives and the Tonga Capability Standard occur, discuss and provide feedback and agree on strategies for improvement as soon as possible. This may involve bringing forward or conducting extra progress meetings or developing a performance improvement plan with the job-holder.

IMPACT OF PERFORMANCE MANAGEMENT APPRAISAL

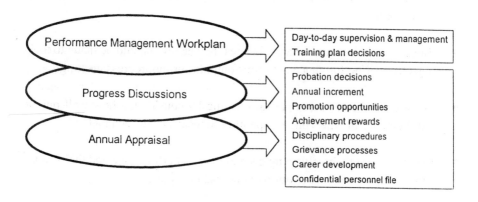

- The Performance Management System Appraisal process ensures that key decisions and career opportunities are linked directly to day-to-day performance.

- The work plan development and progress meetings during the year encourage on-going discussion and feedback between employees and supervisors.

- Training opportunities are targeted to the requirements of objectives and to agreed career aspirations.

- Achievements of outcomes and discussion flowing from the Annual Appraisal impacts on reward, promotion opportunities and any corrective action that needs to be taken to ensure performance is up to standard and disciplinary processes avoided.

DAY-TO-DAY SUPERVISION AND MANAGEMENT

A performance management approach encourages discussion, feedback, coaching and early problem identification and resolution on an on-going day-to-day basis. The planning, progress and appraisal meetings provide formal opportunities to address and record performance achievement.

TRAINING PLAN DECISIONS

The needs of job-holders in meeting set objectives are the first priority in making training budget decisions. Consideration is given to all possible skill development strategies, e.g. working with other job-holders who have needed skill, before making recommendations for formal training.

PROBATION DECISIONS

The Performance Management Appraisal processes provide an appropriate basis for probation decisions. For junior officers, progress discussions and the annual appraisal are brought forward to allow a decision to be made at the end of the six-month probationary period.

For senior officers the results from the appraisal processes are used to determine permanency after 12 months' service.

If the performance is rated E, probation is extended.

ANNUAL INCREMENT

Performance is recognised through the allocation of increments where performance meets most outputs and behaviour standards. Double increments are awarded to high performers.

PROMOTION OPPORTUNITIES

Job-holders whose performance more than meets requirements may be considered for promotion opportunities out of turn and have the opportunity to gain experience through acting opportunities out of turn.

ACHIEVEMENT REWARDS

Job-holders whose performance more than meets requirements are considered for special recognition awards and/or special training opportunities.

DISCIPLINARY PROCEDURES

Performance problems are discussed and resolution sought throughout the year. If at the time of the annual appraisal the job-holder receives a rating of E, a performance improvement plan is developed. The performance improvement plan involves setting of weekly or even daily objectives and close supervision. If, after six months of the next appraisal period, agreed performance outputs and behaviour standards are not achieved, the normal disciplinary processes are followed.

GRIEVANCE PROCESSES

Where agreement cannot be reached by the job-holder and the appraiser during the performance management processes, the issue is referred to the next level manager for discussion and resolution in a joint meeting with the job-holder and appraiser. Issues that remain unresolved are referred to the normal grievance processes through the Civil Service Staff Board.

CAREER DEVELOPMENT

The career development discussion during the annual appraisal provides opportunity for the job-holder and appraiser to discuss and plan personal and departmental strategies to further the job-holder's career development opportunities.

CONFIDENTIAL PERSONNEL FILE

The performance management appraisal processes are confidential between the job-holder, appraiser and senior management as required. During the appraisal year, the appraiser and the job-holder retain an up-to-date copy of the appraisal form. On completion of the appraisal, the job-holder retains a copy, for possible use as a referee report, and the form is retained on the job-holder's personnel file.

PROPOSED IMPLEMENTATION PLAN:
PERFORMANCE MANAGEMENT APPRAISAL PROCESS – TONGA

Activity Area	Tasks	Responsibility	Date
Appraisal Process and Documents	Complete consultation re draft form and guideline	CEO/Establishment and Training Unit	13/08/99
	Changes to master document following completion of consultation	CEO/Establishment and Training Unit	20/08/99
	Inclusion of performance appraisal processes as policy in Estacode	Training and Policy Unit	20/09/99
	Adjustments to policies as required		
	Gaining of approval		
	Development of Special Recognition Award		
Site Preparation	Identification of liaison officers in departments	Training Division and HOD	8/10/99
	Identification of supervisors in Departments	Training Unit and Liaison Officers	9/10/99
	Identification of groups, timings, locations for training		

	Development of support system	Training Unit and Liaison Officers – Information – Materials – Contact lists	November onwards
Training	Develop training proposal		30/07/99
	Develop training – Briefing session activities for very senior staff	Training Unit consultation	
	– Training course for senior managers 1.5 days		
	– Training course for employees 1 day		
	– Train the Trainer in Performance Management Course	Liaise with training Unit on training materials	1/02/2000
	– Conduct Train the Trainers course	Consultant	2/3/2000
	– Conduct implementation training for all participants	Training Unit and Liaison Officers	April/May 2000
	– Conduct performance management training for new employees	Training Unit	Induction program-mes
	– Align Tonga performance management principles with other training undertaken		On-going
	Maintenance of support system	Training Unit – short-term	

		Policy/HRM – long-term	
	Maintenance of policy and master documents	Policy/HRM – long-term	July 2001
	Annual evaluation of overall performance outcomes	Policy/HRM audit	
	Evaluation of performance system	Training Development/Policy/HRM	July 2001

QUESTIONS AND ANSWERS RELATING
TO PERFORMANCE MANAGEMENT

Question 1. **How can high performance be rewarded when they have already reached to top of their salary band and no increment is available?**

The proposed system allows for Promotion and Acting Opportunities out of turn and consideration for a Special Recognition Award. Managers can also use the Career Development section of the process to promote special training opportunities for high performers.

Question 2. **Will Heads of Department be included in the Appraisals?**

Heads of Department will act as appraisers for the managers who report directly to them. Models of developmental appraisals to assist Heads of Departments from other settings are being explored.

Question 3. **What if I find it difficult to mark down a poorly performing employee?**

Training will be given in giving and receiving constructive negative feedback to all participants. In addition, you will have the support of your manager who will countersign the appraisal you give and who can be consulted if difficulties arise in the performance appraisal processes.

Question 4. **How do I develop performance objectives?**

Training in this and other aspects of performance management will be given to everyone before the new appraisal system is implemented.

Question 5. **Can a department add additional behaviour standards for their departments only?**

If there are particular standards that are required, e.g. international health standards or processes, these can be added to the rating. As a first step, it is better to consider if the required standards can be included as a common objective for all employees.

Question 6. **Will developing individual work plans break down a team approach?**

You can include a team co-operation objective and measures/outputs to reinforce team behaviours. In addition, the TCS behaviours include a team factor.

Question 7. **Can we have customers rating individuals?**

90-degree feedback is too complex at this early stage of appraisal system development in Tonga. Customer feedback could be built in by having a separate customer survey and using this to test whether the performance standards on the work plan of customer contact staff were being met.

Question 8. **How will we deal with incremental dates?**

The revised increment form will require managers to refer to the last Annual Appraisal result.

Question 9. **What if my supervisor doesn't like me?**

The system has been designed to be highly transparent and reduce bias. In addition, the Next Level Manager can be called in by the employee if they are not satisfied with appraisal processes. If the issue cannot be resolved, it will be referred to a Civil Service grievance mechanism.

Question 10. **What happens when an employee transfers?**

The supervisor completes an appraisal with the employee when they leave the unit. A new work plan is then developed with the new supervisor who does the annual appraisal with the new employee in July. Both appraisals are combined by the Next Level Manager in deciding Annual Appraisal outcomes for the employee for the Appraisal Year.